TALKING TO YOUR KIDS
IN TOUGH TIMES

WILLOW BAY

TALKING
TO YOUR KIDS
IN TOUGH TIMES

How to Answer
Your Child's Questions
About the World We Live In

WARNER BOOKS

An AOL Time Warner Company

Warner Books, Inc., 1271 Avenue of the Americas, New York, NY 10020

Visit our Web site at www.twbookmark.com.

 An AOL Time Warner Company

Printed in the United States of America

First Printing: September 2003
10 9 8 7 6 5 4 3 2 1

ISBN: 0-446-53326-2
LCCN: 2003107690

Contents

Acknowledgments

There are some friends who, as the saying goes, even if you haven't seen them in a while can pick up right where you left off. And then I've discovered there are some friends who go one step further—picking up right where you left off and pushing you in an entirely new direction. This book would not exist without a friend like that, Laura Yorke. As a mother, she recognized the challenge today's parents face. As an agent, along with her partner, Carol Mann, she seized upon what she believed was a timely idea. As a writer, she offered strategic advice. As my informal editor, she tweaked and tugged. She was the perfect blend of nurturing, demanding, patient, and supportive through this, my first journey into print from television news. I cannot thank her enough.

I'd also like to thank my expert editor, Amy Einhorn, who knew just how to rearrange the pieces into an infinitely better whole. I'm extremely grateful, too, for the efforts of my editorial assistant, Erika Euler. She brought to this project a keen intelligence, boundless energy, and infectious warmth and eagerness. Erika, my extremely talented colleague Tim Braun, and a team of researchers including Rachel Ortiz, Allison Agsten, Amy Fierstein, Felicity Strachan, and Jennifer Maguire worked on a dead-line as tight as any breaking news story we've ever covered. I could not have gotten this book to press on time without their help. And as most working mothers know, behind every good woman is a truly great nanny. And I need to thank mine, Holly McManus Lothian, for the long hours she spent with my children while I worked on this book.

I'll always be grateful to the psychologists, academics, researchers, principals, and teachers who shared their wisdom with me. Their commitment to the physical and emotional development of children is both inspiring and reassuring. To the mothers and fathers who shared their stories and offered a glimpse into the emotional lives of their children, I owe enormous thanks. In a world where a feeling of connectedness to our country, community, neighbors, and at times even family is hard to come by, their generosity forged common bonds. And to any one who reads this book, their stories act as a hand extended in friendship.

And most of all, thank you to the very special men in my life. My husband, Bob Iger, who casually tossed out an idea one night over dinner, was the inspiration for this book. And when I became that lady who sits at the computer downstairs rather than Mom, he pulled double duty with love and grace. The other men in my life, my two sons, were the motivation for the book. I set out on a quest for knowledge that would help me become a better parent—more understanding, supportive, and responsive to their needs as they make their way through this always challenging and sometimes frightening world. I truly hope this book helps them as much as it has helped me.

Foreword: Childhood Threatened

Children worry even when they don't look worried. Every week of their lives, kids are apt to come up with new reasons to feel vulnerable. The sensitive handling of a child's worst fears occupies a lofty niche in parenting, yet there are no predetermined formulas for dealing with all the haunting and daunting preoccupations of childhood.

Mothering and fathering are always mysterious gambits of trial and error performed over years of benevolent experimentation. But the job is never a more anguishing challenge than it is during tough times. And these are tough times. At no point in our history have kids lived amid such a loud, buzzing swarm of threats that confront them with stark clarity and unrelenting immediacy. Life is an emotional stress test for today's youth. The encroachment of war, kidnapping, terrorism, fatal disease, school-based violence, and street crime are not romantically chronicled in the tales of your grandfather in front of the fireplace. Nor does retrospective reporting or hearsay hold exclusive rights to the communication of such threats. The demons now make house calls: They invade your living room (and, in 65 percent of cases, your bedroom), and the deluge comes up on a screen just as soon or almost as soon as they commit their destructive acts.

We cannot turn our backs on what's actually happening, on the unprecedented scenes that infiltrate the psyches of contemporary children. So some urgent questions must be posed and answered: How will this unremitting onslaught of threatening possibilities influence the current generation of kids? How can parents minimize the toxic effects of overexposure to potential danger? How can mothers and fathers provide the most appropriate running commentary to soothe the gnawing anxiety? How can they prevent their kids from either overreacting or, alternatively, becoming oblivious or retreating from the cold truth? It takes well-crafted words and it takes more than just words. Parents need to put in place policies, practices, and actions that enable children to not only survive and thrive mentally but also to grow as they cope with this unique species of adversity—not your normal adversity, but the far more insidious and often more penetrating wounds inflicted by *potential* danger. These are child-rearing challenges that we simply cannot neglect, and they are dealt with head-on within the pages of Willow Bay's book, *Talking to Your Kids in Tough Times*.

While going through this volume the reader will find what amounts to a job description for parents during a stress-saturated chapter in the history of childhood. This is also a manual that can guide them to make the right decisions so they can perform well in this daunting job. The role to be assumed actually amounts to that of the parent as protector. It is an assignment that demands the highest skill and sensitivity. What are the principal components of this job description?

First, parents have to become terrific listeners and observers.

Above all, know thy child! There exists no universally effective game plan, no approach that will work right for all kids. How well you handle them is tied to how well you understand them. This message comes across vividly from the perspectives of Willow Bay and all the impressive experts she consulted in creating this book. There are all kinds of minds out there, and different minds handle stress differently. Some of them harbor fantasies that are far more emotionally lethal than any realities, while others are master practitioners of denial and diversion. So a parent has to fulfill the role of an astute diagnostician, figuring out for each child his way of handling stress as well as the extent to which he processes the nuances of language accurately and deeply enough to grasp explanations and recommendations. Misconstrued messages may be more damaging than no messages at all. Parents also need to decrypt the child's current conceptualization of the outside world and its threats. Where's she coming from? What are her worst fears? What does she think she stands to lose? How imminently threatened does she seem to feel? Parents have to wonder about and act upon these questions. Most of the time they are in a position to respond effectively to support a child. When they arrive at an impasse, they may need to seek professional guidance.

Mothers and fathers should acquire some knowledge and fine-tune their intuitions regarding child development. They need to be aware that the minds of young children undergo progressive change, that they think and react in new ways as they ascend through the years of preschool and elementary school (and beyond). *Talking to Your Kids in Tough Times* offers much sage advice on what thoughts kids are likely to be thinking at specific age levels and how we can conduct our job as their protectors from threat to meet the needs of a particular kid at a particular time of life.

Parents have to mobilize their very best communication skills to counsel their kids effectively. Children are acutely sensitive to our choice of words, tone of voice, body language, and sentence structure. They try to see through what you're saying and how you're looking to obtain a sharp image of what they think you're really thinking. In helping children understand and handle the threats that pervade tough times, it is important to be realistic but not alarmist, to acknowledge the daily dangers while coming across as reassuring without being patronizing. Whenever we brashly admonish a child not to worry or in some other way belittle his worries, we inadvertently put down that kid and persuade him to keep his problems to himself forever after—the last thing we want to see occur! If a child reports that a peer in school is ruthlessly bullying him and a parent simply advises that child to ignore the aggressor, the terror he experiences has been deemed illegitimate. That's not helpful; that's just a parent shirking responsibilities. And that's a little kid who may never again confide in anyone. Bullying can have the same level of impact on a child as being fired from a job has on an adult. We should never cease taking their perspective. A parent's language must project understanding, respect, and support. It is always better to sympathize than to sermonize.

The parent as protector needs to be a formulator of family strategies and policies. This book will get you going. It is a one-of-a-kind compendium of constructive tactics that can be deployed to help kids survive the looming hazards of their world. Whether or not you should talk to strangers, where you turn and what you do in the face of possible kidnapping, how much

TV you watch during a war are among the policy issues that every parent as protector needs to ponder so as to provide rational guidance to children. In all such policymaking, a degree of moderation is called for. There is much to be lost by overreacting to the threats. We don't want to see our kids grow up with deeply embossed mistrust of all strangers and a malignant sense that the world beyond home and school is one vast terrorist cell plotting their demise. We certainly don't want them to think that every stranger is strange. Acquiring a foundation of fundamental beliefs in the goodness of humanity has always been an important ingredient of healthy child development. Willow Bay and her seasoned experts deliver well-tempered advice aimed at achieving a balance between safe caution and a belief that humanity is basically well meaning.

I don't think we ought to overinsulate and isolate our kids; they grow by learning to cope with what's out there. They have no choice but to face and deal with the reality of the times they live in, even if they would prefer to submerge themselves whenever they can in instant messaging, computer games, and other convenient forms of anesthesia. Let's become their consultants on ways of coping—another key item in our parent-as-protector job description.

Greek mythology vividly describes the Gorgons, three monstrous sisters, immense and hideous creatures with huge boarlike tusks and serpents for hair. The Gorgons lived on the edge of the world and were objects of horror to both gods and mortals. Most important, the Gorgons possessed glaring eyes, and those who gazed into their depths would forever turn to stone. Our kids are growing up with more Gorgons than childhood has ever before known. They have to face these threats realistically, but we cannot stand by and see them paralyzed by their fears. We must not allow this generation to turn to stone! Willow Bay has compiled on these pages a reality-based approach that will inspire and enable us to help kids find their ways through the tough times. And, who knows—if we play our cards right, perhaps many of them will actually turn out to be toughened by the tough times.

—Dr. Mel Levine
   Professor of Pediatrics,
   University of North Carolina Medical School
   Director, The Center for Development and Learning
   Founder and Cochairman of the Board, All Kinds of Minds

Introduction

The morning after the first U.S. strike in the war against Iraq, I was curled up in bed with my boys, surrounded by a pile of the morning papers. My four-year-old picked up *The New York Times* and examined the front cover. The headline that day read BUSH DECLARES START OF IRAQ WAR; MISSILES SAID TO BE AIMED AT HUSSEIN. The photo underneath was a fiery red circle dotting the city skyline of Baghdad: an explosion lighting up the dusky skies. My oldest son eyed it curiously and asked, "What's that, Mom?" The war, in my house at least, had officially begun. And the questions—about the war and everything else the adult world hurls his way—were only just beginning.

Welcome to the world of our children where even a morning cuddle in Mom's bed brings news no child should have to confront. And welcome to the world of today's parents where new morning rituals include turning over the papers to hide the horrors on the front page, and turning off the TV morning news.

"Mom, what's a terrorist?" "Dad, did they catch Osama bin Laden yet? Is he coming here?" "Was Saddam Hussein a bad kid?" "If I play with a toy that says 'Made in China' on the back, can I

get sick? Can I get SARS?" "What do soldiers do? Are they good guys or bad guys?" "Are we going to get bombed by Iraq?" "Why do people want to hurt us?" "How long can a person survive without food and water?"

These are real questions from real kids—the kind parents are confronted with every day. All too often they leave us speechless. Remember "shock and awe," the name the U.S. government gave to their bombing campaign in Iraq? It is perhaps a better description of parents' reactions to some of these questions. Sometimes the words and phrases coming out of the mouths of small children make your jaw drop in amazement: Where did she come up with that? How does he know about SARS? How in the world am I going to answer that one?

Kids have always asked lots of questions; they're curious. But parents have never been faced with questions like these. We are a nation dealing with the messy aftermath of the war in Iraq, and a war against terrorism we've not yet won. September 11 changed life as we knew it here in this country, shattering the innocence of a nation and unleashing the fears of both parents and children alike. Now, we live under the continued threat of further terrorist attacks. And there's plenty more to be worried about, homegrown horrors with the "Made in the USA" label on them—Elizabeth Smart, Columbine, snipers, Cipro, dirty bombs, smallpox, potassium iodide—all are part of our vocabulary today, and all are part of the vocabulary of our children.

Other generations have faced crimes and frightening events, but they didn't watch these events unfold in their own homes—in their living rooms, bedrooms, kitchens. The power of the media in our lives today is enormous. It's become such an integral part of daily life that we often do not realize just how potent a force it is. And we all too often underestimate its impact on our children. Television can and did bring us live, in real time, onto the battlefields in Iraq. It brings us right into the home of a family struggling to cope with a devastating loss. A 24/7 news and information culture can exaggerate the real threats we face, and reports of each new threat help paint a picture of the world as a scary place.

These are challenging times for all of us, and they are particularly tough for people raising children. Every time I mentioned this book project to parents, they had a story of their own to share from one of their children. Usually, they had a few questions of their own, too: "So how do I answer?" "Now what do I say?" At the park, at school, at soccer games and dinner parties, everywhere I go I run into parents, eager, and sometimes even desperate, to find answers to their children's questions. As a journalist I want to know the answers. As a mother of two boys I need to know them.

There's plenty of advice out there. For example, on the government's website www.ready.gov Secretary of Homeland Security Tom Ridge says, "Disasters can be pretty scary subjects to talk about, particularly with children . . . but it has to be approached with care." Meaning what exactly? The amount of research into the ways children respond to traumatic events can, in the words of one researcher I spoke to, "fit into a thimble." In the wake of the events of September 11, which traumatized so many children, the mental health community leaped into action. As a result, there is some compelling new research about what parents can and should do when children experience traumatic or frightening events, and there's more on the way. In the chapters that follow I'll bring you the best of what's available.

But what about getting you some help with your child's tough questions? How should you answer? What should you say? What kind of language should you use for a three-year-old? A seven-year-old? A nine-year-old? I could not find that kind of information anywhere. So I went directly to the experts themselves. I started with real questions from real kids. What I discovered was while there are as many ways to phrase a question as there are children to do the phrasing, some common themes emerge. And it's those core fears and concerns as much as the questions themselves that parents must learn to address. I brought all those questions—the same ones your children are probably asking—to professionals who are trained to talk to children. I visited the front lines, talking with principals, teachers and school therapists in communities hard hit by terror, as well as clear across the country. I met with the heads of child development institutes, such as New York University's Child Development Center—in the wake of September 11, the source of a great deal of new research, treatment, and educational materials for parents and teachers—and I contacted doctors who coordinated the treatment of students after the deadly shootings at Columbine High School. I contacted key researchers studying the impact of violence and the media on our children. And I spoke with therapists who talk one on one with children every day. They all had answers—lots of them. In this book, I've also collected what I think is the best of their advice. And in some cases, I've road tested these answers for you when the topics came up with my sons, so I know the advice really works.

QUESTIONS—YOURS AND THEIRS

This book is written for parents of children ages three through nine. Although they have been expressing their needs and wants for some time, around the age of three children's developing language skills allow them to begin to express their emotions, too: fears, concerns, and worries. By age ten children are beginning to enter preadolescence. They have the cognitive maturity and the coping skills to handle the world of adults more effectively than younger children. It is these in-between years where they really need our help to make sense of the world around them.

Preschoolers ages three through five will certainly come to you with questions, fears, and concerns, but typically they have an easier time dealing with the adult world than elementary-school-aged children. Most young children have much less knowledge and awareness of the world outside their own little universe, and can be shielded from the adult world more easily. It's the ages of six through ten that are a bit more challenging, because children at this age are exposed to a great deal of what goes on in the adult world but lack the cognitive maturity to make sense of it all. In addition, they don't yet express their emotions the way adults do, and that makes it tougher for parents to read what's going on in their minds. Our children may be far more sophisticated than we were at their age, and they are certainly exposed to far more, but they are not "little adults." As parents we need to understand this before we answer their questions. When I can, I provide specific ages or age ranges for this information, but I'm not always able to do so. This is a guide for parents, not a cookbook with precise recipes: *bake at 350 degrees for forty-five minutes* will not always apply.

Which brings me to another important point. As any parent knows, all children are different. They grow, learn, and interact with the world in their own unique ways. What your child does at two, my own might accomplish at three or four. So to use the cookbook analogy again, take these age recommendations with a grain of salt. You'll know where your own child fits into the ranges.

ANSWERS FOR YOU, AND FOR THEM

I'd love to offer parents a book filled with all the "right" answers, but of course there are none. There are as many ways to answer a question as there are parents and children, each with their unique mind and heart. What I can do is offer tools that I've collected from experts in child development, psychology, and early childhood education for parents to use to create a conversational comfort zone where children feel safe asking all kinds of questions, especially the scary ones. This is a place where parents feel comfortable too—where they are able to manage their fears and help their children to handle theirs. These are tools that will help parents get past that initial moment of panic that sometimes sets in when we are confronted with questions we really don't want to have to answer.

As I've researched this book I've come to believe that parents—despite their own anxiety—often leap too soon to answer children's questions. We want to teach, inform, make sure they've got it right. But what we need to do is to get better at listening, observing, digging a bit into the minds of our children. We must understand what they know, what meaning they arrive at from the information they have, and what they need to know in order to make sense of what is going on around them. We have to help them to manage their feelings about it all. In order to do all this, we must develop our investigative skills—observing, listening, asking the right kinds of questions—before we give answers that provide knowledge, comfort, and reassurance. These are the kinds of skills that as a journalist I use every day at work. I'm now learning how to use them at home.

My goal with this book is to help parents turn a communication challenge into a communication opportunity, and turn tough times and tough questions into "askable" moments that will in the years ahead add up to a lifetime of conversations with their children. As one mother of three boys told me: "The subject matter isn't going to get any easier so we might as well figure this out now." As with many of the other thoughts from mothers, fathers, and experts that I'll share with you in the pages ahead, I could not say it any better myself.

PART I

Children's Fears— Big and Small

Why Parents Panic

IF YOU WERE DESIGNING a world in which it was easy to raise kids, you wouldn't pick the one we're living in here in America. If you wanted certain material advantages you'd pick this one, but if you were trying to make it easy on parents you wouldn't." When I heard Robert Evans, a clinical and organizational psychologist and director of the Human Relations Service in Wellesley, Massachusetts, say this, I felt a sense of relief. No, it's not just my imagination, being a parent *is* harder than it used to be. Raising children is challenging, exciting, and rewarding. It has always been that way. But these days it has become an increasingly complicated and nerve-wracking task.

It's clear parents are shaken by the world we live in—and the world our children will grow up in. We're often startled by the questions our children are posing and many of us are struggling to find the "right" answers. And it leaves me wondering: Why is this so hard? Is it a problem that's unique to this generation of parents—a sign of the times we live in? Are we missing skills that our parents had? Do we need new parenting skills for these new times?

WE LIVE IN SAFE TIMES THAT FEEL SCARY

We are the safest nation in the world, living in the safest times in our history. Nevertheless, these safe times often feel very frightening. It doesn't seem to make sense. Statistically speaking we live longer, healthier, more protected lives than ever. Our life expectancy, for example, has risen considerably in the last decade alone. Scientific and technological breakthroughs have reduced risk in nearly every area of life. Yet, one of the consequences of the information age is that we contend with a tidal wave of information about potential danger—from scientists, the media, and even our own government. We consume a near daily media diet of warnings of danger. There are scores of new products designed to keep us safe, but also myriad product liability lawsuits to compensate us for injury. Remember the hot McDonald's coffee? Who knew we were in grave danger from the contents of a styrofoam cup? Similarly, the medical community trumpets breakthrough cures for illness even as it uncovers new diseases. Is it any wonder we're anxious?

As if all of that were not enough to keep us on edge, we have the all-too-real memories of the worst terrorist attack in U.S. history. September 11 shook this nation to its core. We now have new color-coded security alerts from the Department of Homeland Security that will warn us of the level of risk from a terrorist attack. Operation Iraqi Freedom, as brief as it was, also raised new fears that involved bioterrorism or chemical attacks. And this country, vowing never to be caught off guard again, remains on alert for additional terrorist attacks—biological, chemical, or nuclear. We are facing new threats as a nation. And we are facing new demands as parents.

NEW THREATS FOR NEW TIMES

Of course each generation faces its own set of dangers and has to deal with them. I didn't do "drop and cover" drills in school as did children of the Cold War era. And while I'm sure that my parents tried to shield me from news reports about the Vietnam War, those reports came neatly packaged on the nightly news. They were not available in real time, live from the battlefield twenty-four hours a day. "Even during other wars," says Diane Levin, author of *Teaching Young Children in Violent Times: Building a Peaceable Classroom,* "the media was not such a presence in family life and childhood. It was not constantly bombarding us."

Memories from our childhood, and the parenting we received (back in the days when it was called raising children), guide us when we raise our own children. We act on instinct shaped partly by those early memories. At times, we do as our parents did. (How many times have you said to yourself, "I can't believe I said that. I sound just like my mother!") And at times, when we have unpleasant or unhappy memories about the parenting we received, we intentionally do just the opposite. "You use a lot of your own experience as a child that's just kind of embedded in your consciousness or subconsciousness," Levin explains, "but here we have a whole new set of threats to our safety and the safety of our children to contend with. This is a place where parents have not had anything in their past to help them deal with it, so they don't have anything embedded in their prior experience." In the case of some of the new twenty-first-century threats we are facing, we simply do not have the guideposts from our own childhood to show us the way.

More than a lack of guideposts, we no longer have a road map. Increasingly, in this country, we create our own path through life, no longer following the one our parents took. Evans offers this explanation: "It's harder to raise children than it ever was because most of what we associate with advances in American life is actually making it harder to know how to raise kids. Most of the world lived, and still does, in settings where there are relatively few choices for a child's life, and therefore there is a high level of certainty for the adults raising him or her. In a primitive fishing village—the men fish, the women dry fish—you have a son or daughter and you know what they have to learn. There's no choice of a career but there is high certainty of parenting. We flip that around. Any kid in America should be able to become anything and live any lifestyle—freedom is high, but consequently the predictability for an adult is very low. And the world keeps changing—just five years ago if you had a kid in college who was heading into high tech, you'd have been very happy, because you would have had no idea that the technology sector was going to crash, that the companies were going to go bust, and there'd be a 25 percent vacancy rate in the San Francisco Bay area." Similarly, just five years ago who would have imagined a toddler talking about planes crashing into buildings—real planes? Or having to sign permission slips allowing your child's school to give her potassium iodide tablets in the event of nuclear fallout from a terrorist attack? Or watching a security guard search your child's backpack at a Yankee game?

Just as our world is changing, so are our families, and our neighborhoods—two of the anchors we rely on as parents. According to Bureau of Labor Statistics, seven out of ten women with children under age eighteen worked outside the home in

2001. More and more parents leave children with caretakers, nannies, relatives, or in daycare. Increasingly, our neighbors do the same. "There's nobody left to do the homemaking—I don't mean that in an Ozzie and Harriet sense, I mean to make the house a home. I don't care who does it or how they do it together, but we have fewer places where that happens," Evans notes. He adds, "We have people reinventing the wheel because nobody lives in a neighborhood anymore—even if they're fairly close to another house. We don't live in places where if I see your kid misbehaving outside my house, I go speak to you. And I can't count on you to do the same if my kid's misbehaving. So we're each left more alone to do this, more on our own. It's hard to know how to parent kids."

CRISIS OF COMPETENCE

The time we spend on our careers enriches us intellectually, socially, emotionally, and financially. But we do spend less time with our children, and as a result we are less familiar with the world of our children. And often, we are less comfortable in that world. It has been a gradual change that Evans says teachers began noticing years ago. "I worked with a lot of preschool teachers, and when they have parents come in for a day to play with the kids, there are a lot more parents who have a hard time just playing with the kids. They can teach them something, they can coach them, but they can't just sit at the dollhouse and play with them comfortably. So while the career sophistication we have gained is really remarkable, it has come with a certain price in terms of child rearing savvy." What happens in times of crisis, and in times that are troubling, is that parents are far less sure of themselves, less confident in their abilities as parents. And as Evans points out, in many cases we have much less experience on the playground or the playroom floor. Evans's diagnosis? "There's no question in my mind that there's an epidemic among parents—a crisis of confidence and competence."

In addition to the fact that the world we are raising our children in is very different from the one in which we grew up, there are some universal truths about parents that make parenting today more difficult. For the most part, as parents we want to control the world our children live in. We want to protect our children from harm and we also want to protect them from feelings that are uncomfortable, frightening, or difficult. When we're faced with questions that tug at our hearts or give us knots in our stomachs, we want to make those feelings disappear. This has always been true of parents.

In the face of all this—the uncertainty of a rapidly changing environment, new threats for which we have no precedent, the absence of familiar anchors of generations past, less familiarity with the world of children—is it any wonder that we sometimes panic when our child asks a question about one of these "new" threats? Wendy Mogel, a clinical psychologist and author of *The Blessing of a Skinned Knee,* offers another sign of a lack of confidence: "We want experts for everything. We want experts for psychotherapy to fix our children. We want the very best art teacher and the best math curriculum and the best reading program in school. And then we want the best answers to children's questions about war and drugs." Of course we do. We want the answers and we'd like them quickly. Expediency and efficiency are signs of the times, right?

Parents are eager for help, even for someone else to tell them what to do to be a good parent. And that's exploited in many ways in our culture. "Just look at how toys are marketed," says Levin. "You can buy this crib toy for your six-month-old. The baby can push a button and the toy recites the letters of the alphabet. You'll give him a head start, and help your child learn to read. And what parent wouldn't think, 'I want to give my kid a head start?' But the reality is that toy could actually undermine your child's learning to read. At this age babies benefit from interacting with the real physical world. It's a foundation for all future learning." Pushing those buttons is a meaningless activity at this age. We want to raise our children to be problem solvers rather than button pushers.

Parents have an understandable, even commendable desire to "get it right." And when a child comes to us with a question that makes her frightened, worried, and anxious we are even more determined to make sure we get the right answer. "Parents are so afraid they're going to make a mistake if they talk to children about important issues," explains Mogel. "But the fact is that kids' knowing that you're there to talk to them is probably more important than anything else."

As a parent you will be faced with a lifetime of questions—and some of them will be troubling. You'll come up with answers—lots of right ones and probably a few wrong ones. But it's establishing the process that's important, and that's what this books aims to accomplish for you. Every expert I've spoken with has said you can always go back and try it again, and say to your child, "You know, I've thought about it a bit more . . ." Parents don't always have to have the right answer right off the bat.

Children are extremely resilient. They need to know we are

there to listen. They need to know they have a comfortable and safe place to go with their feelings and questions. They need to know we are available to go there with them. Children have always needed these things. But in today's world where adult concerns invade the lives of children, they need it even more.

Parents today need to work a little harder to help our children navigate the world they live in and to create a safe, comfortable place in which they can ask us all sorts of questions. Kids do not need perfect answers, but they do need a parent giving them some answers.

So while I'll offer plenty of advice to help you understand your child's fears and your own, I'll also offer plenty of techniques you can use to encourage conversation. I hope you'll take a deep breath, relax, and learn to enjoy this very meaningful and very rewarding part of parenting. It is hard, but the important things in life usually are.

Our children will in all likelihood be facing a whole new set of issues as parents. They'll be asking us how we survived what we did in much the same way we asked those questions of our parents. Think of how often we've joked about the childhood dangers we lived through. How did we turn out okay when our mothers smoked and drank during their pregnancy? As we consider the merits of car seats with the new "latch system" or the ever so crucial five-point harness, we should remember that when we were little, we didn't wear seat belts, we sat in the front seat or we climbed all over the back, often with a bunch of other kids and the family dog. And look, we made it! We survived. Despite the challenges we face it appears we are thriving. And the reality is, despite the larger threats against us, so will our children.

Television: Too Much of a Good Thing

IN APRIL 2003, during the war with Iraq, a seven-year-old boy asked his mother, "How do they get the salt to stick on those guns?" "What guns?" she asked, clearly confused by the question. "The salt rifles," he replied. At that point, the mother realized her son had heard a news report about the AK-47 assault rifles used in the war. But it's not only violence that captures our children's attention. During the Monica Lewinsky presidential scandal of 1998, a first-grade boy informed his parents at breakfast one morning: "Mom, Dad, we need to talk about what's going on at the White House at dinner tonight. I just don't get it." After his parents spent a day figuring out how to explain oral sex and presidential liaisons to their seven-year-old, that night, at dinner, the boy finally asked: "Look I know there are interns at hospitals, but why are there interns at the White House?"

These are just two stories out of hundreds of thousands in which children pick up bits of information about current events from the things they see and hear on television, radio, and the

Internet. Our children are the first generation in the history of the world who are able to get huge amounts of information that's not filtered by their parents or teachers. And we are the first generation of parents to raise children exposed to this much-uncensored data. Perhaps most unsettling is that so much of what our children see and hear comes from the television sets in their very own homes.

TELEVISION—IT'S JUST NOT WHAT IT USED TO BE

The images of television are more intensely affecting than the printed or spoken word and offer less context. Everyone—adult or child—pays more attention to things that move. We humans are wired that way. If you are reading a book, totally engrossed, and a mouse runs across your living room floor, you'll notice that tiny moving image.

Regardless of content, there is a built-in magnetism to television. But in the case of television, children inhabit an entirely different universe from the one their parents did. Robert Evans explains, "A kid with a television in his room can watch as much news on Iraq as he wants, and his parents aren't paying attention. And a kid at his computer can mess around with as much pornography as he wants." Those are just not the kind of opportunities for trouble we had as children. Most of us grew up in homes that had one television set. We got up and walked over to the set to change the channel. We watched as a family. A parent usually controlled what we watched and when. Not anymore.

Children have far greater access to television today. Forty-eight percent—nearly half—of U.S. television households have three or more sets. That means a lot of children are watching alone in their rooms. And they often watch without a parent to provide context and explanation. There was no CNN when we were children—now there are half a dozen live news channels available twenty-four hours a day, seven days a week. Add to that the proliferation of media of all sorts—magazines, newspapers, radio, and the Internet—and it's clear that our children are growing up with unprecedented access to news and information.

All of us who live with this steady barrage of readily available information today know how powerful the media are. Acknowledging this power has almost become a cliché. And we can blame any number of social ills on it. But managing it, and truly understanding its influence, requires a bit more effort. "The media are more powerful than we even realize," says David Walsh, founder of the National Institute of Media and the Family, a nonprofit organization based in Minneapolis. "Not good or bad, but powerful. Good or bad depends on how it's used. And because the media are powerful and because they occupy a larger and larger role in kids' lives, it becomes more important that we make sure that we use them for benefit and not harm," he adds.

So what are the media habits of the average American family? Walsh and his organization developed the MediaQuotient survey tool to measure family media habits. The parents in these homes recorded their own media usage and reported their own observations of the effects on their children. According to MediaQuotient, a survey of families with children ages two to seventeen, the average American child:

- Watches twenty-five hours of television each week.
- Plays computer or video games for seven hours each week.
- Accesses the Internet from home for four hours each week (for those who have Internet access).

In addition to studying how much media children consumed, the MediaQuotient survey also asked parents the following questions about how those media were used in people's homes:

	Always	Often	Sometimes	Rarely	Never
How often families have a TV on during meals	18%	22%	26%	18%	16%
How often families have a TV on even if no one is watching it	*	27%	27%	27%	19%
How often children watch educational TV	8%	39%	39%	11%	3%
How often children see parents read	*	65%	25%	7%	3%
How often children have TV on while doing homework	4%	12%	14%	22%	48%
How often children copy characters they have seen on TV	*	15%	35%	32%	18%
How often parents monitor how their children use the Internet	52%	15%	12%	8%	13%
How often parents talk to their children about the music they listen to	*	48%	34%	12%	6%

*Not given as a possible option.
Source: National Institute on Media and the Family.

According to a study released by the Kaiser Family Foundation, an independent organization that conducts research projects on health care issues and the impact of media in society, two-thirds of kids eight and older have a television in their bedroom. Also troubling is the fact that 61 percent of children eight and older say that their parents do not have set rules about television watching. The study also revealed that parents watch television with their child just 5 percent of the time. And younger kids, too, are increasing their media use. The Kaiser study showed that for kids in the two- to seven-year-old range, 32 percent have televisions in their rooms and parents are watching programs with these kids only 19 percent of the time. The following statistics suggest parents could be more effective gatekeepers than they are now:

Percentage of kids who have a TV in their bedroom

All kids 2–18:	53 percent
2- to 7-year-olds:	32 percent
8 and older:	65 percent

Parental oversight

Percentage of kids with no rules about TV:	49 percent
Percentage of homes where TV is usually on during meals:	58 percent

Percentage of time parents watch TV with their kids

2- to 7-year-olds:	19 percent
8- to 18-year-olds:	5 percent

Source: This information was reprinted with permission of the Henry J. Kaiser Family Foundation of Menlo Park, California. The Kaiser Family Foundation is an independent healthcare philanthropic organization and is not associated with Kaiser Permanente or Kaiser Industries.

A NOISY MEMBER OF THE FAMILY

In many ways the most intensely affecting of media—television—has become another family member, a steady and often noisy presence in our family life. Television has been called "electronic wallpaper," the "electronic hearth," and the "electronic babysitter." Whatever you want to call it, it is neither comforting nor benign. Having the television in the background has a profound effect on everyone in the room, especially children. Parents tend to underestimate not only the amount of time their children spend consuming media but also just how much of it their children absorb whether from within their homes or from the world around them. Too much television viewing and the wrong kind of TV watching affects children physically, emotionally, and psychologically. A substantial body of research suggests these negative effects include low school performance, increased aggression, and the prevalence of symptoms of psychological trauma. Walsh also believes too much television contributes to the growing problem of obesity in American children. Recent studies show that children with a television in their rooms, for example, have a 31 percent greater risk for obesity. Why? Kids with televisions in their bedrooms watch more of it at the expense of other activities, such as riding a bike. Although there is not much data on the issue yet, it's not a leap to assume that too much time in front of a computer screen or a video game console isn't too great for kids' waistlines either.

Media diets high in violence have been shown to increase aggression, fear, desensitization, and appetites for more media violence. When the television program *Teenage Mutant Ninja*

Turtles was popular, "We saw more aggressive behavior on the playground," says Ruth A. Peters, clinical psychologist and author of *Laying Down the Law: The 25 Laws of Parenting*. Preschoolers karate kicking their way through recess may not exactly be cause for great alarm, but it is a direct, clear example of how a child in preschool or early elementary school mimics aggressive behavior he sees on television—even in a "harmless" kid's cartoon. "A steady diet of television violence nourishes a culture of disrespect," says Walsh. "We see more unruly behavior, bullying, and rudeness on the playground as a result." How many times have we heard the complaint—teachers are spending more time managing students' behavior in the classroom than they are teaching? Too much of the wrong kind of television may be partly to blame.

Of course, not all television is bad. Educational television, such as the educational programs shown on PBS, can actually generate positive effects in children's lives. For example, according to Joanne Cantor, professor emeritus at the University of Wisconsin-Madison and an internationally recognized expert on children and the mass media, research has shown that "the more kids watched *Sesame Street* in preschool, the higher their grades were in high school." She also commends *Blues Clues* for its lessons in critical thinking and *Mr. Rogers* for its proven positive effect on children emotionally. There's also a large body of evidence suggesting that educational television teaches prosocial attitudes such as nonsexist and nonracist beliefs. It can also teach reading, math, science, media literacy skills, emotion recognition, and empathy. Barney, the irritating purple dinosaur aside, Elmo, Dora the Explorer, and the "tween" craze of the moment, Lizzie Maguire, are just some of the characters on children's television that are boosting vocabularies, broadening world views, and teaching positive life lessons to the children who tune in. However, even too much nutritious food is unhealthy, and the same is true for "too much" good TV.

HOW TV NEWS AFFECTS OUR KIDS

But what about children who are exposed to television news? What is the effect on them? Diane Levin, who has studied the impact of media on children for more than twenty years, told me the following story about a mother and her daughter, who was having trouble sleeping at night. Although it was the fall of 2001, she, the mother, believed her child, Sarah, was simply having a hard time adjusting to daycare. The mother was convinced that she'd completely sheltered her daughter from the coverage of the terrorist attacks of September 11.

"About a month after September 11, when planes were flying again in her community, a plane flew overhead at daycare, and the child ran under a tree. Later that day, Sarah's teacher asked her mother if the child knew anything about what happened in New York. Sarah's mother said, 'Oh, no, no, no. I've protected her from all that.' And the teacher said, 'I'm wondering because this is what happened today. You may want to ask her.' So the mother said to Sarah, 'Have you heard about anything that happened in a place called New York?' Sarah replied, 'Yes, Mommy. Some bad guys crashed a plane into a building and it fell down.' Suddenly it dawned on the mother, it wasn't daycare that was keeping her daughter up at night. She asked, 'Sarah, have you been thinking about that sometimes? Is that why you're getting up at night?' And Sarah said, 'Yes, Mommy. I'm scared that a plane will go into our house.'"

TV producer Susanna Aaron says she felt September 11 was an important historic event that she wanted her five-year-old son, Sam, to witness. "My feeling was—rightly or wrongly—he wouldn't be traumatized. The TV was on the whole day and I let him see it." About a month later, Sam started having nightmares—sometimes two or three a week—about a boat crashing into their home. She says, "That's when I knew I had maybe gone too far." She would talk to him right after the dream, asking him to describe it, "Tell me about the room we were in, who was with him, did we die—and we didn't. In fact, we weren't even hurt. If you think it through with a child, it demystifies the fear."

That was in New York City, but as far away as Los Angeles, one eight-year-old boy was swimming in a pool not long after September 11, heard a plane overhead, and asked his mother, "Do I have to get out of the pool now?" When she asked what he meant, he said, "Are those good planes or bad planes? Maybe I should get out of the pool."

Parents repeatedly discover that children pick up far more from television than we realize, and still we're always a bit surprised by this fact. "I almost crashed the car," says designer Cynthia Rowley, when her three-year-old started to tell her about how "some little boy had a gun and pointed it in some other boy's face. I asked her if she meant a toy gun or a real one? A real gun. When I asked her where she'd seen this, I found out it was from watching *Montel Williams* with her nanny. I put a stop to that kind of TV right away." What they don't get from TV, the odds are high they'll hear from another child and then pass along. "They may not pay attention, and that's great," says Dr. Robin Goodman, director of New York University Child Study Center's website, AboutOurKids.org. "But that doesn't mean it hasn't crossed their radar screen. Even if you turn off the television sets in your house, children hear things from older kids, they see the pictures on the covers of the newspaper, and they see the television on in the corner deli and in the doctor's office. They hear and see all sorts of things. So to believe you can protect them from this is foolish."

Diane Levin has grown increasingly interested in news violence and its effects on children; she has recently revised her book, *Teaching Young Children in Violent Times: Building a Peaceable Classroom,* to include the impact of news violence. Levin says it's very clear that children get ideas about the world from what they see and hear on television—both news and entertainment. They are more likely to "tune in" to news accounts that include their interests, such as animals, planes, or snowstorms, and things they can identify with—other children, for example. Consequently, violent heroes have more of an impact with children than violent villains (just ask the toy marketers), because children identify with heroes. They want to dress like them—in Superman pajamas, Spiderman Halloween costumes—and act like them.

Young children under the age of seven often don't yet distinguish between "real" news events and entertainment television. Levin explained, "When they're young and they see things in the news, they'll bring what they see to try to understand or interpret entertainment. And when they see entertainment, they'll often bring it to try to understand the news. Children, for example, watching the events of September 11 on television, said it looked like the movie *Independence Day.* My own son, who was nearly three at the time, saw a replay of the event and said, "Planes crashing—that's crazy!" Another three-year-old thought the towers were hurt: "Building fall down. Building need a kiss." For kids, the images were exciting, puzzling, and disturbing. What they were missing, of course, is the underlying meaning of the terrorist attacks, reacting instead to the single dimension of "how things looked."

But are the effects of news violence similar to the effects of entertainment violence? "The news does not glamorize violence in a way that action movies, television programs, and video games do," says Walsh. "But it does have an impact on kids." Television news provides a window on the world, but a rather distorted window. It can create what Walsh refers to as "the mean world syndrome," a world with more crime and violence, for example, than the world most children live in.

So are children able to distinguish between entertainment and news programming? Do they understand the difference between real-world violence and violence meant to entertain? "Basically—seeing is believing—it doesn't matter if it's news or entertainment," says Cantor. "From the point of view of a four- or five-year-old, learning the difference between what's real and what's make believe is a very gradual process and, usually, it takes until they get to the ages of six, seven, eight before they can sort out the difference. A good example of this is the Wicked Witch of the West in *The Wizard of Oz.* She's extremely frightening—she looks frightening, she's mean and has a squeaky voice. And until kids are seven or eight, they don't understand that there's not somebody like that who's going to get them."

Younger children, usually those under five years, also have little grasp of time and geography. Young children have an undeveloped sense of time, space, and cause and effect. They cannot yet understand the relationship between action and consequence. Toddlers and preschoolers watching news coverage of September 11 believed that planes were hitting the towers each and every time they saw a replay. A six-year-old child in Los Angeles was also very preoccupied with planes. When his mother started to question him about this she discovered he wasn't worried about his own safety, but extremely concerned about his grandparents. He was fearful that the planes were headed to Washington, D.C., where his grandparents live. He knew that a plane had crashed into a building there—the Pentagon—and thought it was going to happen again. He was convinced that his grandparents' house would go up in flames. Although they live in the suburbs about twenty miles away, in his mind it was right next door.

What young children—children as young as one—can do is "pick up" the emotion of television images. A one-year-old baby, for example, will become upset when exposed to television programming that shows lots of conflict, emotion, and aggression. We know that babies and children respond to the emotions of the adults around them, but research suggests that even babies will respond in a similar way to televised emotion. "Young children will sense there is an emotion," explains psychologist Ruth Peters, "but will not be able to interpret what that emotion really means. They recognize that someone is having feelings, and may wonder—should I be having feelings? Which ones?" As a result, toddlers and preschoolers can be quite affected by television coverage of news events that parents believe is outside their grasp. Walsh believes that between the ages of five and seven, children begin to distinguish between news and entertainment. And somewhere between the ages of seven and nine it begins to become clear.

What's also clear is that children pick up an enormous amount of misinformation from television news coverage. All children, of course, process news events in different ways, which is why we hear so many questions that make little sense to an adult. For example, a six-year-old girl told her parents she planned to be a reporter when she grew up and travel the world. But then she asked: "Would that mean I had to go to places like Afghanistan, Pakistan and . . . *Taliban?*" Parents need to acknowledge that children pick up bits and pieces of information and make their own meaning of them. Frequently, it's only after a parent unravels this meaning that the child's fear becomes clear.

SIDE BY SIDE: A LESSON IN TV WATCHING

Adults are all too aware of the daily assault of information. But imagine, if we struggle with it in our daily lives, how our children are struggling to manage the bombardment of adult information in a news culture that reports more bad news than good, and more frightening stories than inspiring ones. Moreover, children are coping using less mature intellectual, emotional, and social skills than we have as adults. "Trusted adults have a vital role to play helping children feel safe and sorting out what they hear and do," says Levin. "I would go on to say we really border on being irresponsible for not taking the importance of this job seriously. I don't think it's intentionally irresponsible, but I think we have a responsibility we are not assuming adequately to help children process news violence and violence in the world. I think that when children hear about these things they try to figure out what they've heard. They have reactions of fear, excitement, anxiety, and they need to learn that adults are there to help them figure these feelings out and to work it through and answer their questions, and reassure them about their worries. I think they need to view us as helpers alongside them in dealing with this stuff. Children really need us to sort this out. But right now I think very few children have that opportunity."

When we watched TV on the couch alongside our parents, we had this opportunity all the time. We may not have recognized how healthy it was for children to be sharing those experiences with a parent. Today, we have to work to create those opportunities. Michael Cohen, a psychologist and father, says he tries to help his daughter with her weekly homework assignment using *Time* magazine for kids. He helps her understand the news and he gets a valuable opportunity to understand just what his daughter knows about current events. It's a great way, he believes, to connect to her world. Similarly, the parents of a nine-year-old "news junkie" get up early on Sunday to watch the news programs with him. "He knows more about the Middle East than most adults," his mother proudly admits. But she, too, knows a great deal about her son—about what he understands and what he may not, about world events.

Despite the advice from the experts that children under six should not be exposed to news coverage at all, I do allow my four-year-old to watch it occasionally—with me sitting next to him. Sometimes, at six-thirty at night I'll say to him: "Let's see what's going on in the world." And we'll tune in to the network nightly newscast together. While I am getting caught up with the latest policy change by the current administration, or the latest vote on the Senate floor, he's learning that Mr. Bush is our president. He has two houses: the White House and one in Texas. The latest financial crisis for one of the airlines is, for him, a chance to indulge one of his passions: airplanes. Obviously, during the war with Iraq, for example, or when extremely frightening events are in the news, we don't watch. And I don't watch the local news with him. (I actually do think local news is far more sensational and thus frightening for children, despite the allure to a young boy of helicopter chases and firemen putting out blazes.) I know what the rules are, what the experts say—no news programming for children under six. But it's an informed decision that I make—informed by what I think my child can handle. I really do enjoy sharing that brief look at the world with him. And he seems to benefit from the experience.

MONITORING MEDIA USE IN YOUR HOME

The experts I talked to agree: Parents need to monitor children's television viewing more than they do now. Here's a look at how the parents in the MediaQuotient survey monitor their children's media use:

- Only 58 percent of parents have rules about how much TV may be watched.

- Only 34 percent of parents "always" or "often" use the TV rating system to help them select what programs their children may watch.
- Only 40 percent of parents "always" or "often" look at the industry ratings before buying computer or video games.
- Only 26 percent of parents with Internet access use a blocking device for children's Internet use.

Unfortunately, that's just not good enough. "We have to re-think a lot of what we do given the role of the media in our children's lives," says Levin. Because the media occupy a larger and larger role in our lives, and in the lives of our children, parents need to work harder to maximize the benefits and minimize the harm. Levin believes that parents need to help children sort out what they watch, read, and hear from the media. In particular, parents need to help children deal with the violence they see, providing guidance, reassurance, and support.

WHEN TO TURN OFF THE TV

By now, we all know the basic guidelines: Do not watch the television or listen to the radio while your children are present. Don't discuss the alarming news of the day while children are around. This is the most basic piece of advice for parents. It's not only specific viewing that affects kids—the TV's constant presence weighs in, too. John P. Murray, a Kansas State University professor who has conducted brain-scan studies on children as they watch television, explained to *The Wall Street Journal*, "It becomes background but it does not go away. It doesn't mean your body isn't responding and that your brain isn't respond-ing." Many experts believe the biggest mistake parents make is to assume that their children aren't paying attention to the back-ground noise of television.

It turns out that turning off the TV might not be such a bad idea for adults, either. About a week into the war with Iraq in spring 2003, *The Wall Street Journal* reported on the effects of the war playing out as background noise in our homes. The ar-ticle suggested that the health risks for adults associated with regular television exposure to traumatic events include increased risk for depression and stress and weakened immune systems. Excessive war viewing before bedtime can cause stress, induce nighttime snacking, and interfere with sleep. Some researchers believe that the type of stress triggered by disturbing television images is more harmful than the type of stress we face on the job. Research done after September 11 suggests that passive stress, such as that experienced while watching TV, can take a greater health toll. As James Garbarino, author of *Parents Under Siege,* adds, "Several studies suggest that the more TV you watch, the more unsafe you feel, and the more unrealistic your view of what the dangers are and where they come from. The world seems more threatening. It's one of the reasons parents are increasingly anxious."

TV IN A CRISIS

So what should you do in a crisis, when adults want and need news and information and when children are not supposed to watch? Parents learned a great deal during 9/11. I know I learned from my mistakes. As the events of September 11 unfolded, I did what most Americans did—and what broadcast journalists instinctively do in times of crisis: I turned on the television set. Craving information of any sort to make sense of the unimaginable terror and tragedy, I remained transfixed for days. As a West Coast–based financial news reporter for CNN, I was largely left out of the coverage of events in New York and Washington, which only made my need for information more acute.

On that Tuesday, I kept my son—then nearly three years old—home from school. Somehow the forty-five-minute drive in Los Angeles traffic to spend two hours in a playground just did not make sense. So home we stayed—he with his toys, and me with my TV set always on—in another room, of course, but always on.

In those few days, television shaped our collective experience. TV journalism may have been at its best, providing information and offering solace to a devastated and frightened nation. But in the experience of children, I was to learn that the very same medium could be quite harmful.

When I came to pick him up after his first day back at school, I asked his teachers how to respond to his questions about the terrorist attack. His teachers asked me: How does he know about what happened? I told them he'd seen a bit of it on TV. Their unequivocal response? Turn the TV off and keep it off. With at least twenty years more experience with three-year-olds than I had, his teachers weren't the least bit sympathetic to my personal need to stay up to date as the horrible events unfolded. They were even less sympathetic toward my professional need to stay informed. Preschool teachers are in the business of nurturing young minds and bodies as they grow and learn. And all good teachers are—as are I'm sure your own children's teachers—extremely committed to protecting the world of childhood as a haven for growth and learning. On that day, his teacher was adamant and even stern in letting me know what was best for a preschooler: a total news blackout. Why? Because in addition to the obvious fears that news accounts can cause, as we've learned, children have no ability to distinguish a "live" event from a replay of the same image. They live in the present, so every time they see the image of the planes hitting the towers, it is a brand new crash in their minds. And young children have such keen radar that they sense emotions of adults—more than that, they can pick up those emotions from TV. But whether their homes had a news blackout or not, within a day or so the toddlers at my son's school were drawing pictures of the event, building towers with blocks and knocking them down and chatting in incomplete yet horribly clear phrases about planes, buildings, fires, and crashes. While experts say turn it off, here are ways some other parents handled those fateful days:

• One New York City mother let her four-year-old son watch *some* of the news on September 11 because, "I remember when Kennedy was shot. I was a little older than three. I remember my mom at the back door of school, and she was very sad. She looked at me and said, 'The president has been shot.' I remember understanding how important that was to her because I'd never seen her so somber or upset. That memory stays in my mind and I'm happy to have a memory of a moment so pivotal in our culture."

• On the other hand, one Washington, D.C., mom didn't

allow her two boys, ages five and six, to see any of it. As a child, she'd seen pictures in *Time* magazine during the Vietnam War—images of soldiers carrying the decapitated heads of the Vietcong that remain seared on her brain. "Now I make sure the news is never on," she says, "I have since my son turned four. I TIVO Peter Jennings to watch when they are in bed."

We know what the rules are, we know what the expert advice is: It's best to shield young children from this kind of news coverage. With the war in Iraq, I did just that. I kept the TV off. But, if there were ever again an event as profound as September 11, I might decide to share some of that news with my sons. Every parent needs to make a decision that's right for her and one she believes is right for her children.

MEDIA GUIDELINES FOR YOUNGER CHILDREN (UNDER SEVEN)

Turn the TV off: Look, believe me, I know this is hard. As one former *Today Show* producer and father to three children under the age of seven told me in dismay, "We don't even watch the *Today Show* anymore!"

With young children, it's best to curtail media use. There is just no reason they need to watch. The American Academy of Pediatrics recommends that children under two watch no television at all. The organization says that there's no evidence that educational TV is good for children under two, but plenty of evidence that what babies really need to do is interact. Needless to say, "the electronic babysitter" doesn't qualify.

Take the television set out of their bedroom: This is perhaps the most radical piece of advice, and upsetting to your children if they already have a TV in their room, but one that also makes the most sense. It is easier to monitor a child's television viewing if she is not watching it alone in her room.

Choose educational TV: Parents who report their children "always" or "often" watch educational television are less likely to report that media viewing has had a negative effect on their children.

FOR OLDER CHILDREN, AGES SEVEN TO TEN: A MANAGED MEDIA DIET

While that may work well for small children and it is ideal to protect them from events they cannot begin to understand, a news blackout is neither possible nor appropriate for children of all ages. With older children the news provides opportunities to engage in conversation, explore issues, and connect with the world around them.

Set limits: Set limits on content and hours watched on television, along with limits on video games and Internet use. It is very hard to find specific, consistent recommendations for how much television is healthy or reasonable for school-age children. The American Academy of Pediatrics recommends limiting television viewing for children ages five to twelve to an hour or two daily. *ScreenSmarts,* a family guide to media literacy produced by Wisconsin Public Television, recommends a maximum of ten hours a week. Walsh, at the Center for Media and Family Studies, who advocates a "managed media diet," recommends the following limits:

- Children under two: none to very occasional.
- Children two to five: no more than five to seven hours a week.
- Elementary school: ten to twelve hours of screen time (TV, video, and computer games). Computer use for educational purposes doesn't count.
- Junior high and high school: twelve to fourteen hours (following the same guidelines as for elementary-school children).

While I feel very strongly that parents should monitor their children's TV viewing, I know it's tricky. In a family with children of different ages, it's even harder. Despite the AAP's guidelines of "no TV" for children under two, I let my one-year-old watch Nickelodeon alongside his older brother. I can't quite figure out how to satisfy the needs of all the children in the family. Do you insist your nine-year-old watch only programs that are acceptable for your five-year-old too? How do you do that math, if that same five-year-old is allowed five hours of TV a week, and your nine-year-old is allowed seven? The limit may be optimal for your child's well-being, but let's face it, sometimes it's just not practical. Every parent has to develop a routine that makes sense for the entire family—and that may mean breaking the "rules" now and again.

Watch the news with your children. Assess how they are processing the information they receive. The academic researchers call this "coviewing," but it's really how we used to watch television—with our parents. You can watch some news programming with children over the age of six. (Children ages three to five are just not ready to process news—or any adult—programming. And yes, I know, this is the rule I occasionally break.) "But parents should be careful," says Cantor. "If the story suddenly turns to child abduction—and even if the kid seems to be paying attention to something else—those kinds of things will attract kids. Then the parents will find themselves having to reassure the kid that he won't be abducted."

Talk: Parents who talk to their children about television programs are also more likely to report the media having a positive effect on their children. The more you watch television with your children, the more you'll help them to understand the adult information they receive. When children are a bit older, eight, nine, ten, this is a great way to begin to develop "media literacy," an understanding of how different forms of media, in this case television—shape the stories we see.

Encourage alternative activities: Encourage reading, sports, anything other than sitting in front of the computer or television.

Yes, I know I am motivated in part by self-interest—television news has been my career for nearly a decade. And in our home, where one parent works in the news business and another one is an executive managing news and entertainment divisions of a large media company, there's just no way we could be antitelevision. But, I really don't think "No TV" is a good idea for children. I also truly believe that it is impractical and even undesirable to deny your child access to television in a world where it so shapes our pop culture. It deprives kids, too, of the fun of learning the alphabet with Big Bird, or solving mysteries with Blues Clues. That's why I like the "managed media diet" philosophy advocated by Walsh and others. Its goal: to minimize the harm and maximize the benefits of media exposure. It suggests looking at television as you would food. It's important to find an optimal balance of the right kinds and right amount of television for your child, just as you would with food. The same is true with "good" or age-appropriate TV. Establishing limits on both quality and content will help to achieve that balance.

Fears of Childhood

FEAR—IN CHILDREN and adults—is a normal and healthy part of human life, a biological response to a perceived threat. But, in children, sometimes that response can be puzzling.

It was the Fourth of July 2002, families were gathered to watch the fireworks display from a pier overlooking the ocean on the Maryland shore. One boy, age eight, there with his own family, was as excited as the rest of the kids. But the moment the fireworks began, he started to scream at the top of his lungs. He took off—running down the beach. His parents chased him, but lost him in the crowd. Later the police got a call from a woman who lived down the beach from the pier. She had found the child standing outside her door, shivering and disoriented. When the police arrived, they found him inside her home sitting in a chair, happily watching the fireworks through the window. His parents were relieved, but completely stunned by his severe reaction. Their son was usually an easygoing, relaxed child. He'd never been afraid of fireworks before.

What happened that caused the boy so much fear? Clearly, this response to the fireworks was more than a "typical" childhood fear. After all, he was eight, not three, when you might ex-

pect a child to get frightened by loud noises or bright explo-
sions. So what triggered the severe reaction? What caused him
to run for the "safety" of a stranger's home? It turns out the boy
had been traumatized by the events of September 11 and responded to the fireworks with extreme fear. But those were the
kinds of questions his parents had to answer, and the kinds of
questions all parents face when a child's fear—mild or extreme—is a mystery to them.

In this chapter, we'll explore children's fears from the "typical" fears of childhood, often called "developmental" fears, to
the more severe ones caused by the intrusion of the adult world
into our children's lives. We'll also look at signs that a child's fear
has become unhealthy—much like the sniffles that turn into
bronchitis—and requires the help of a mental health professional.

LIFE'S EARLY CURVEBALLS—THE "NORMAL" FEARS OF CHILDHOOD

As a parent, you'll probably remember why an eight-month-old
baby suddenly screams when the neighbor whom she cuddled
with happily a few weeks ago picks her up. It's classic stranger
anxiety. But did you ever wonder why your four-year-old races
for the box of Band-Aids at the first sign of a scratch? Or perhaps your seven-year-old calls home from his after-school play
date and gets the answering machine. When he gets home he
lashes out verbally, "Mom I called and you weren't home. You
scared me. You were supposed to be there!" Do you wonder
what all the fuss is about?

Childhood fears are a reflection of developmental milestones. Fears in children are likely to appear in a developmental sequence. Understanding this process will help you identify and manage typical childhood fears. Jacqueline Haines, director of the Gesell Institute of Human Development, an education and research organization in New Haven, Connecticut, which publishes that wonderful series of books on childhood development called *Your Two Year Old* (and *Your Three Year Old*, *Your Four Year Old*, and so on), says the behavior children exhibit has a direct correlation to neuromotor development, physical changes in the brain. "If you watch children's behavior it can act like a television camera on the brain," she adds. So if you want to know what they fear, start by watching how they behave.

Here are some of the basic healthy fears, and the age at which they typically appear. These are some of the building blocks of a child's cognitive development.

INFANTS AND BABIES

Infants are typically frightened by surprises to their senses. The world, and all its sights, sounds, and experiences, is brand new to them. Loud noises, bright lights, and unexpected movements can cause fear in an infant. From six months to two years, babies—like the eight-month-old mentioned above—typically display stranger anxiety and separation anxiety. But did you ever notice that when you are overloaded and stressed out by too much on your plate, your baby is suddenly *more* demanding of you, clinging fiercely and not playing contentedly in her playpen as usual? That's probably a sign that she's picking up your anxiety. Babies at this age are able to sense the emotions of their caregivers and react in response. This "emotional radar" continues to develop as children age.

TODDLERS: AGES EIGHTEEN MONTHS TO THIRTY-SIX MONTHS

At this age children have begun to interact with a broader physical and social environment. At around two years old, some children begin to worry about their physical safety and develop fears about such common activities as swimming, bathing, or going to the bathroom. A toddler may worry she'll disappear down the bowl when she flushes the toilet. Or she'll worry that she'll be swallowed up by the drainpipe in the street outside her house. A friend's daughter at eighteen months spent all summer splashing in the water. Six months later, on a vacation to Mexico, she refused to go in the pool and screamed hysterically because she was so afraid. While this can seem baffling and even infuriating to a parent, child psychologists will tell you it's perfectly normal.

PRESCHOOLERS: AGES TWO TO FIVE YEARS

By the time children are this age, they usually have become part of a social group beyond their family. Their language, play, and social and physical skills are more advanced. From two to five, children are "extremely egocentric" says Dr. Harold Koplewicz, professor of clinical psychiatry and pediatrics at the New York University School of Medicine and director of NYU's Child Study Center. They demonstrate pride in all the things they can do with their bodies, but often develop fears about injuries and pain. They know things can hurt them but aren't sure which ones.

So that four-year-old who rushes for the first-aid kit at the first sign of a scratch may be compelled by more than the thrill of opening a new box of Bob the Builder Band-Aids. He may be worried, for example, that all the blood will leak out of his body. Kids at this age may become victims of their own vivid imaginations.

Children ages two to five have very specific fears, which may include:

- Separation from parents or caregivers
- Their own health and the health of a parent
- Dogs, bugs, clowns
- Death
- Disaster
- Pain
- The dark

At this age, through their budding language skills and play, kids can begin to express their feelings of anxiety.

SCHOOL-AGE CHILDREN: AGES SIX TO TWELVE YEARS

By ages six to twelve, children's fears are often a mix of the unrealistic or imaginary (tigers, dragons, and things that look "scary") and may be centered on bodily harm. Kids fear threats to their homes, such as fires and burglars, and threats to their parents. They also begin to fear threats outside their homes, such as the threat of kidnappers. They begin to fear the unknown—their death or the death of a loved one. Fears of school failure, and daily anxieties, such as being called on unexpectedly by a teacher, become very realistic concerns. Children become more independent and are able to talk about their thoughts and feelings, but their anxious moments mean they'll often want to stay close to their parents.

By about age seven, issues of fairness become very important. This is the age (particularly ages seven through nine) of living by the rules. Children see the world in very black and white terms, and do not understand subtleties and nuance. While many parents with children who stay up past their bedtime might say their children love to break rules, in truth breaking the rules makes children uncomfortable. Children use those rules to help them order the world and cope with anxiety. That seven-year-old who couldn't get his mom on the phone became frightened when she wasn't there. In his mind, she was "supposed" to be home. All the logical reasons why she was not standing by the phone waiting for that call are lost on a child of that age. She had broken the rule. And it made him feel anxious. Here's another example of a child of this age bound by rules: A seven-year-old girl in New York became very agitated when she arrived at school one day and a substitute teacher was in the classroom. The girl wanted to know where her teacher was, whether her teacher was ever coming back and why her teacher was not there. She became quite upset because it wasn't the way "it's supposed to be."

ADOLESCENCE: THIRTEEN YEARS AND OLDER

By the time they hit adolescence, children's cognitive abilities allow more abstract ways of thinking about the world, and their fears change accordingly. Traditionally, a child who was afraid of scary-looking ghosts and monsters turns into an adolescent who worries about real-world violence that could do her harm.

THE DOWNWARD DRIFT OF ADULT FEARS

As society changes, of course, so does the content of children's fears. Some recent studies of school-age children indicate that children's fears may be growing more adult.

About eight years ago, Patricia Owen, a clinical psychologist at the University of St. Mary's at San Antonio with a research interest in fear, took a sabbatical from her academic work to teach third grade at an inner-city school in San Antonio, Texas. "What I had discovered, among many things, was that these children I was working with had fears that were different from the fears that my own son had had at their age. And those fears were quite a bit different from the ones I had when growing up." Owen decided to take a closer look at those third-graders' fears and began to collect data. One question she had: Are the children of the nineties having to deal with fears that are different from those of children of the sixties and seventies? She explains, "According to normative tables, third-graders, or that age range, are supposed to be afraid of things like monsters, or getting yelled at by the teacher or something like that. And it's not until adolescence or preadolescence that children are supposed to be becoming afraid of real-world fears. But I was finding that my third-graders were very much afraid of real-world fears. These kids are only eight, but they are not supposed to be afraid of these things until they are eleven or twelve."

Owen continued to survey other third-graders in San Antonio, developing a larger database. She studied Anglo and Hispanic children of different socioeconomic groups and discovered their fears were quite similar.

TOP FEARS OF EIGHT- AND NINE-YEAR-OLDS*

BOYS	GIRLS
1. Drive-by shootings	1. To die
2. Kidnappers	2. Drive-by shootings
3. Gangs	3. Nuclear weapons
4. Gunshots	4. Gangs
5. To die	5. Kidnappers
6. Nuclear weapons	6. Earthquakes
7. Strangers	7. Burning
8. Snakes	8. Death
9. Guns	9. Guns
10. Fire	10. Poison

*Among Hispanic and Anglo children of low and middle socioeconomic status.

She then took her survey on her travels, studying children of the same age in Cambodia, Burma, Indonesia, and Mexico. Some fears she discovered were culturally based. Kids in America fear drive-by shootings, while children in Indonesia have no cultural equivalent. But some fears occur in all the samples, and are what she calls "universal" across gender and cultures. Nuclear weapons, death, and kidnapping appear as top-ten fears in every country she studied, and in every socioeconomic group. So far her research has confirmed her earlier hypothesis—that children of eight or nine are facing fears that older children and teens would have faced years ago.

What's of greater concern than the content of their fears (and clearly it's troubling that eight-year-olds are worried about drive-by shootings) is that children are confronting these very adult fears with the emotional and intellectual capabilities of eight-year-olds. It's a question that concerns Owen. "Are those young children cognitively mature enough to understand and cope with these fears? Are they emotionally equipped? If these fears are reaching kids at younger and younger ages, the big question is can they cope? And I don't think so. I don't think they have the cognitive maturity. So you might see other indications that they are struggling with that fear: somatic symptoms, changes in sleep, they might be more distractible, have problems concentrating, maybe lethargy," she says.

A more recent study by the Education and Research department at Sesame Workshop, the nonprofit educational organization best known for creating *Sesame Street,* came to a similar conclusion in a project called "A View from the Middle: Life through the Years of Middle Childhood." The study involved children of different backgrounds in the six to eleven age range from various parts of the United States. The research began in May 2000 and concluded in May 2002, nearly a year after the terrorist attacks of September 11. The researchers had children document their own view of the world through essays, drawings, and photography. Originally, they hoped to gain a better understanding of the needs of this age group for educational programming, but the study yielded much more. They discovered children live with a great deal of fear. Among their most common fears were guns, death, and violence. The results point to the presence of adult concerns in the minds of children, what Sesame Workshop refers to as "adult sprawl."

What's surprising and disturbing is that children reported these fears *before* the terrorist attacks of September 11, 2001. When asked about their worries, nearly two-thirds of the children gave vivid descriptions of violence against themselves or their families. Among nine- to eleven-year-olds the proportion was greater than three-quarters.

- "My worst fear is a gun. I'm afraid of being shot because of things happening in the world today."
- "I'm afraid of a bad guy holding a gun and facing it towards my mom and dad. I don't want them to die."
- "I'm afraid of being killed. I hear weird sounds outside my window like a pecking sound."
- "I'm afraid of strangers. They take you away."
- "I know there are a lot of dangers when I'm out in the world on my own."

The researchers concluded that the fears of these children "reflect a mainstream epidemic transcending geography, race, income level, and gender."

Owen's work with third-graders and the Sesame Workshop study suggest that—like so much of the adult world—grownup fears are spreading to the world of children. Adult sprawl, downward drift, age compression—whatever label we give it, the burden of adult fears on young minds is a significant problem for our children, and a real challenge for us as parents.

Susan Royer, the vice president for Education and Research at Sesame Workshop, says children report being frightened by day-to-day violence, and they say they feel very alone in their fear. Children feel assaulted by the news, and worry that they are not safe. Among their other fears: their environment. These children voiced concern about the deterioration of the places they play: parks, playgrounds, and indoor play spaces. Children "saw this as a sign that adults weren't terribly mindful of their needs." Royer says, "They sense parents aren't paying attention and it frightens them." Children of this age group do not want to burden their parents with their fears, but they do want and need to be listened to and comforted by adults.

Another major concern of children in this study is a widespread concern of many children today—much the same as it was when we were young—bullying. Children are mean to each other, sometimes they are physically aggressive—pushing and shoving. And more often they are abusive mentally—gossiping, backbiting. You've probably seen it with your own kids or their friends at the playground; it starts at an early age, and even the little ones will say, "I don't want to play with you today," or, "You're not my friend anymore." Dr. Kyle Pruett, a clinical professor of psychiatry at the Yale Child Study Center, tells the story of a preschool boy who brought duct tape to school and refused to part with it. He heard it would protect him. He wasn't going to use it to seal up a room—he thought it would keep him safe when the class bully picked on him.

Our kids have to handle so much each day—school, friends, sports. And they display such ease with many of the trappings of adult life. Do you remember how young your children were when they began to load the VCR themselves? My son can work a sophisticated audio-video touch screen (a plain old remote control is considered an antiquated relic in our house) with shocking ease. It's hard not to forget sometimes how little they are. And it's hard to remember that the fears we had at their age are probably their fears as well—will her best friend want to play with her at school today or will she choose someone else? Will the teacher call on him in class and embarrass him when he doesn't really get what's going on? Or will he be buried under what feels like an avalanche of homework?

What the researchers at Sesame Workshop discovered in the follow-up phases after 9/11 is startling. When they compared all three phases of the study, the kids felt more anxious and vulnerable in May 2000 than they did right after September 11. And eight months after the terrorist attacks of September 2001, children expressed less preoccupation with violence than they had two years earlier—before 9/11. The number of children who wrote, "My family keeps me safe," or, "Home is safe," tripled by the final phase of the survey. The fears the children expressed were most widespread and dramatic at a time adults would describe as peaceful.

According to Sesame Workshop, children are more disturbed by everyday threats or routine violence than by war or terrorism.

So what happened in the lives of these children that would make them feel safer and less fearful during one of the more terrifying times in this nation's history? Why did kids across the country report feeling less frightened and anxious when their parents were in all likelihood frightened themselves and worried about more terrorist attacks, anthrax, smallpox, dirty bombs, and the threat of war? The researchers at Sesame Workshop believe that children may have benefited from the extra awareness of their needs after September 11, 2001. Attention from parents, extended family, and teachers helped children deal with

9/11, as did signs of united communities and families. Howard Kudler, an associate clinical professor in the department of psychiatry and behavioral science at Duke Medical Center, reached a similar conclusion. He says data collected from both a New York City and a national sample indicate that while an extraordinary number of children were distressed, they did not develop a mental disorder in response to the events of September 11. The vast majority of children recovered quickly in large part due to the efforts of their parents. "What 9/11 taught us is that parenthood works" he says. "Parents did a good job at being supportive, providing important facts and showing their kids by example that they were resilient. Parents were certainly upset by the events, but they were not destroyed and their children followed suit." In countless ways, parents got on with their lives—returning to work and normal routines. Children watched and did the same.

As much as children pick up information from the world around them, and as much as they get from television, the information they get from their parents resonates more powerfully. "Children watch their parents more closely than they do television. Parents matter more," Kudler adds. Dr. Robin Goodman agrees: "Kids would rather get answers and information from their parents than from anyone else," she says. I have heard the same thing from mental health practitioners over and over again.

After September 11, most parents focused on the needs of their children. They stayed close to home physically and emotionally. Together with the larger community—schools, town, cities, and the country—they created a sense for their children that "no matter how tough this is, we are here for you, and we are in this together." That's a message that helps children in times of crisis. But it is also a message that will help them get through the less traumatic but very real fears of daily life.

TYPICAL SIGNS OF FEAR OR INCREASED ANXIETY

Just as there are typical developmental fears—along with the more adult fears—that a child may have, there are some fairly typical responses to those fears. A child may display signs of increased anxiety in her behavior at home, in school, or with friends, and a parent needs to consider the intensity, duration, and age appropriateness of the behavior as well as its effect on the child's everyday activities. Some signs of increased anxiety are:

- Sleep disturbances or nightmares
- Bedwetting
- Changes in eating—eating too much, or not at all
- Being easily startled and jumpy
- Inability to concentrate
- Withdrawal from family and friends
- Physical complaints with no apparent cause, stomachaches
- Refusing to go to school, excessive clinging
- Irritability
- Aggressive play
- Sadness, listlessness, or decreased activity
- Preoccupation with death, violence, safety of parents

Here are some of the ways this behavior might appear in children of different age groups:

- *Infants:* Infants have a limited variety of responses to fears. They cry when startled by loud noises, sudden motion, or bright lights. They cling if they sense they are falling.
- *Toddlers:* Common reactions include increased tantrums, clinging, changes in eating, sleeping, and bathroom habits.
- *Preschoolers:* Same as toddlers. Expect a fair amount of regressive behavior. For example, a child who mastered separating from a parent years ago may suddenly have a hard time. Look for changes in play, drawing that might include more aggressive behavior, or reenactments of frightening scenes. Worries about "who" did it, and what will happen to them.
- *School-age children:* A need to stay close to parents; inability to participate in normal activities, such as play and schoolwork; increased aggression and problems at school; insomnia or nightmares; changes in eating habits. Perhaps your eight-year-old is complaining of stomachaches and says she doesn't think she can go to school because she feels sick, but she has no other signs of illness and flu season is over. She may not want to go because she is worried, or frightened of something. Maybe your nine-year-old's grades are dropping. He's having problems concentrating on his schoolwork. That too may be a sign that he is worried or anxious about something.

Robin Goodman says parents may misinterpret symptoms: "A mother at home with her children may say, 'The kids are fighting more. They are driving me crazy. I just can't stand it. They are just at that age . . .' So when children are fighting and irritable, parents may assume they are fighting and irritable. Well they may be not just at that age. That may be a sign that they are not able to manage things internally." A parent needs to know what is typical for her child. Does she usually fight with her brothers and sisters? Are there certain things that trigger irritability—such as a lack of sleep? In this case, trust your instinct and investigate a little further when things just don't seem quite right.

KNOW YOUR CHILD

While the age and developmental stage of a child are important to understanding her fears and how to manage them, understanding your child's temperament is also critical. As any parent knows, children emerge from the womb with a unique temperament. It expresses itself in those first few moments of life: how he cries, reacts to light, sounds, and the warmth and smell of his mother's body. While siblings may look alike physically, they rarely have similar personalities. We begin to understand that temperament at birth, and our understanding of it, deepens throughout a child's life.

"I think it's the obligation of parents to start understanding who your child is," says Dr. Koplewicz, who describes the unique temperaments of his own three children: the "hothouse orchid," the "easy, giving soul," and "the politician." Understanding a child's temperament is key to understanding how she handles her feelings, and when she's having trouble managing them. A child's temperament helps determine what is *normal for that child*—a combination of actions parents recognize as typical: how she eats, sleeps, learns, and socializes. For example, one child, when she meets a new person, may avert her eyes, look down at the floor, curl a foot inward. A stranger may think that's unusual behavior (especially if that person has children who are friendly and outgoing), but this may be absolutely normal behavior for that child. It's part of what Koplewicz describes as a baseline for your child: "You know how they eat, sleep, interact with other people. You know what your child is passionate about. Is he obsessed with Buzz Lightyear? Soccer? Painting? That's what I mean by knowing your child."

In times of crisis "typical" behavior might change, and a knowledge of a child's baseline might well help a parent identify a problem. Koplewicz adds, "That's why we have to know our kids all the time, so that when something changes—when there's a death, a stress in school—that we are able to pick that up. And what are we looking for? The signs and symptoms start with basic things: appetite, sleep, concentration, and fun." Some questions parents can ask: Is the child sleeping well at night or visiting your bed more often? Is she having a hard time concentrating on her schoolwork? Not interested in that bowl of spaghetti that used to be her favorite food? Not interested in playing with that Buzz Lightyear doll or going to soccer practice? Does she seem weepier, clingy? You look for signs of change the way you would look for symptoms that would indicate your child was getting sick. And again, you know your child better than anyone else—you'll probably feel that something isn't quite right even if you're not sure what it is.

HOW TO IDENTIFY A PROBLEM IN
YOUR CHILD'S PLAY

The play of children often offers clues to what's going on in their minds. A child will often work through an upsetting or frightening event or issue through games or artwork. For example, children old enough to write will often draw pictures and write a "script" with a positive outcome.

I think the clearest example of this is what children did with blocks after September 11. Across the country, teachers and parents reported children building towers—with blocks, Legos, Tinkertoys—and then knocking them down with pretend planes. After some time (and that amount of time varied), the children moved from knocking down the towers to rescuing the people inside. They brought in pretend police, firefighters, and ambulances to help save the people. That is how they worked through the event. A similar process occurred in the artwork of older children. They drew pictures and wrote captions to tell stories with happy endings. For example, a second-grader in Los Angeles drew a picture of a tall building and a sun shining down on it. Underneath it she wrote: "The buildings fell down. It was a bad day. The sun came out."

But sometimes when a child cannot get past the "destruction" phase, and appears "stuck" or unable to move beyond the initial outcome, she may need some help to direct her play. When an adult redirects a child's play, it is important to involve the child in choosing a new direction rather than providing one. Using the block example, a parent might say, "Gee, those buildings have been knocked down. What can we do to help?" rather than saying, "Here are some fire trucks and ambulances, maybe you can save the people who are hurt." It allows the child to solve the problem on her own and move on.

If after a few days your child continues to repeat the violent or aggressive behavior obsessively, and even with some gentle guidance cannot move on to a more positive or peaceful scenario in his play, that may be a sign he cannot manage those emotions, and a signal to you to ask for professional advice.

WHAT IS TRAUMA? AND HOW DOES IT AFFECT OUR CHILDREN?

People experience trauma when they witness someone dying, or experience a threat to their life or the life of another person. September 11 was for many adults and children experienced as a traumatic event. One can also experience trauma by hearing about a death or significant injury to a loved one. For example, getting a phone call that a loved one has died in a car accident would certainly be considered traumatic. "A traumatic event," says Goodman, "is threatening or overwhelming in an objective way that is different from a fear that a child would normally have—like the fear of separation." Trauma elicits feelings of fear and horror, a loss of control or predictability. People also lose their sense of competence and mastery.

Dr. Bruce Perry, senior fellow at the Child Trauma Academy in Houston, explains, "When a traumatized child is in a state of alarm (because they are thinking about the trauma, for example), they will be less capable of concentrating, they will be more anxious and they will pay more attention to 'nonverbal' cues such as your tone of voice, body posture, and facial expressions."

The message a person gets from the experience of a traumatic event is that "the world is a dangerous place, and I am not competent to manage." So the response to a trauma typically focuses on reversing that message. The new message should be: "The world is safe, or at least safer than it seems now. And you are able to manage." While all children respond to events differently, 9/11 was for many children—especially those in the cities where the attacks occurred—a traumatic event. Many parents in the Washington, D.C., area said the sniper attacks that terrorized them for twenty-two days were far more "traumatic" for their children than even the crash of a plane into the Pentagon. It was far more frightening for many kids and certainly far more disruptive to their daily life.

HIGH-RISK KIDS

If a child is either physically or emotionally close to a potentially traumatic event, he is at a greater risk of being negatively affected by it. So in the case of September 11, a New York City child who lived near the towers or who lost a parent or loved one that day would be at greater risk, as would those who lacked a strong support structure of family, friends, and community.

In addition, children under eleven are at a greater risk to experience trauma. They have fewer ways to express their emotions, so it is easy for a parent to underestimate how much trouble a child is experiencing. They don't have the same ability with language that adults do, so they cannot describe their reaction. For example, "Kids are sometimes irritable, cranky, or angry," says Goodman, but those may also be signs that they are stressed, depressed, or afraid. Children also lack the coping skills of adults. They can't integrate information, nor can they put an event into perspective as an adult can. Adults can manage their fear by telling themselves there's a one in a million chance this will happen to me. But most children under the age of eight or nine don't understand the concept "one in a million." To a child of three, thirty is a big number. Children cannot put an event out of their mind as an adult can. What children often do instead is to master and control a fear through play. Here's an example from the play of a six-year-old boy in Maryland, who during the sniper attacks pulled out his mother's blow-dryer to use as a gun in his game of "sniper." Children have to do very specific and concrete things to manage their fears. Goodman says to look at what children often do with a scary movie. They'll watch it over and over again. Or they'll start it and stop it when it gets too scary. Then they'll try it again. Parents come up with very concrete things to do to help a child who has fears at bedtime because it helps them feel a sense of control: check the closets for monsters, sprinkle monster powder around to keep the monsters away, turn on the light. Children under ten respond to such specific strategies.

WHEN SHOULD YOU LOOK FOR HELP?

Mary Beth Brogan, a specialist in early childhood development in New York City, explains, "The most important thing for a parent to do if they do not know what their child is trying to express is to get help—especially with the younger ones who may not be able to articulate what is wrong, but are just as frightened. Without help, their fears will not go away."

If your child's fears routinely interfere with normal daily activities like some of those mentioned above, it may be a sign that he's experiencing more than a "typical" level of fear or anxiety. This is a very basic guideline many practitioners use. If a child stops participating in normal, daily activity, that may indicate he's developed a phobia—an intense and persistent irrational fear.

Dr. Robert Landaw, a pediatrician based in Los Angeles, characterized it this way: Take a four-year-old who develops a fear of dogs after a neighbor's dog lunges at him. The loud barking coming from the house next door is making him jumpy. That's an entirely normal and age appropriate fear. The child and his mom are walking over to a friend's house, and as they pass the house with the dog he squeezes his mom's hand, tenses up, looks nervously over his shoulder, and keeps on walking. That, too, is an entirely appropriate response that indicates the boy is managing his fear. He's coming up with ways to do that on his own: holding on to Mom, looking around for signs that the dog may be near. If the child refuses to walk up the block past that house, and won't go over to his friend's house to play unless his mom drives him, the parent might want to examine his behavior more closely.

In a more extreme example, after the sniper attacks in Washington, D.C., one eight-year-old boy became so afraid of going into open spaces that he even refused to go to his baseball games, which until then had been his passion. In this case, the child's parents were able to talk about his fears with him and help him feel safe enough again to return to the playing field.

Goodman suggests in a case like this one that the parent observe the behavior and comment on it. "I've noticed that you don't want to go to your baseball game. What's going on?" This may yield some clues to what the child is feeling. Or she adds, "Give the pediatrician a call, and ask does this sound like a problem to you?" This is the time when a parent should really listen to his instinct.

Gail Furman, a clinical psychologist who works with families and children in Manhattan, says, "Ninety-nine percent of the time, you'll spot the problem—you'll see it on their face. Don't let a lot of time go by. For example, if a child is irritable for more than three days just check in with someone—your pediatrician or the school therapist. It doesn't mean the child needs therapy. It often means that a parent needs guidance so he can help his child work through the issues." If a parent needs more help, a pediatrician or a school psychologist can recommend a child psychologist who specializes in the mental health needs of children and families.

Many parents are reluctant to seek help for their children's mental health problems. If your child had a sore throat, and you were concerned that it was a sign of something more serious, like strep, you'd probably call your pediatrician or take her over to the doctor's office. Mental health professionals say that just as with physical problems, the prognosis is better for psychological problems when they are identified early.

EASING CHILDREN'S FEARS— WHAT CAN PARENTS DO?

There are some basic guidelines parents can use in times of crisis, stress, or anxiety that work regardless of the traumatic event. "You can substitute terrorism, bombings, murders, floods, fire, death—almost anything," says Robert Evans. "There are always differences for any given person, situation, and family, but essentially the things that make a difference in helping people, kids in particular, are very similar. It's not like a generic template you slap on something but the core guidelines are not very different." Experts tell us that what works in times of extreme stress, to ease children's fear and provide a sense of security, also works to soothe children suffering from less severe frights as well.

Here are some of the most important things parents can do to care for children—physically, emotionally, and psychologically—during crises, both big and small.

STICK TO ROUTINE

Fears of the unknown are the first to appear in human life, and they stay with us. We rely on the familiar in order to feel safe. A child's first feeling of confidence comes from being able to master her fears of the unknown. The more things stay familiar, the less these first feelings of mastery are challenged. This is why the sniper attacks in D.C. were so traumatic for many children. Their daily lives were turned upside down for weeks. They were locked indoors at home and school—no playing outside at recess, no baseball or soccer games on weekends. Even the walk from the car to the front door of school became—in some cases—a frantic dash for cover. The more a child's daily routine changes, the harder it is for her to develop that psychological buffer of safety which she needs to make her way in the world. This is why children need the safety of predictable routines, and why they turn to the comfort of familiar daily rituals to help them manage their fear. It makes children feel safe to do the same things over and over. Consequently, children have a natural tendency to try to get back to routine signposts of normal life as soon as possible. They look for the familiar and predictable. So, even if your life is turned upside down—as was the case for so many people after September 11—make sure your child's life stays the same. If you usually read *Where the Wild Things Are* or *Madeline* at bedtime, do it now. If your child eats Cheerios and milk for breakfast every weekday morning, give it to her. And if you run out of milk, go to the store and get some. It is these small daily rituals—which may seem inconsequential to an adult—that make a child feel secure. It is also important to take care of children physically in times that are traumatic or stressful: Make sure they are sleeping, eating, playing, and getting enough physical activity. Observe their behavior for the signs of stress.

TURN THE TELEVISION OFF

This is very basic commonsense advice that we often forget. As I discussed in the chapter entitled "Television: Too Much of a Good Thing," as a result of some of the horrors that we have experienced in the past few years, most parents understand how important it is when the news is frightening or violent to turn the television off. In fact, so many parents turned the news *off* during the war with Iraq and turned channels like the Disney Channel, and Nickelodeon *on*, that some children's television networks reported an increase in their ratings. But we are so accustomed to the daily violence of the news—on television and the radio—that we don't really notice the car crashes, robberies, murders, and fires that the news brings into our homes every day. But our children do, and it often makes them anxious. Especially with young children, under seven or so, keep them as protected as you can from news that may frighten them. After seven or so, if you want to allow a small amount of supervised television watching, monitor the content and watch it with them.

LISTEN . . . LISTEN . . . LISTEN

"It's my impression after listening to parents for thirty-five years," says Dr. Pruett, "that when you assume you think you understand what is driving a child's behavior, what's on their mind, what they feel, what they think, what they're responding to, you are more likely than not to be mistaken. That's why it's very important to listen." After a tragic event, children need us to listen even more.

After the shootings at Columbine High School, teachers in Littleton, Colorado, reported that they "felt like therapists." The children had to talk through their feelings so much that they had little time to teach. One minister in Virginia reported that in the weeks that followed the attack on the Pentagon all she had to do was ask a question at her Sunday school groups and the "floodgates" would open. The children had lots on their minds.

How many times have you heard a child whine, wail, or moan: "Mom, you are not listening to me"? How many times have you heard one say: "Dad, I need you to talk some more"? Without question, one of the most important things parents can do for children in need is to listen, and to make them feel as if they have a safe place to go to express their feelings. And while it is certainly critical to listen to a child in times of crisis, it is also imperative that we take more time to listen to our children every day. They need us to, and want us to. In the chapters ahead, I'll offer some ways you can become a more effective listener and create a comfortable place for your child to express thoughts and emotions at any time.

REASSURE CHILDREN THAT THEIR WORLD IS A SAFE PLACE

When faced with a disaster or crisis, children need to be reminded of how safe they are at home, at school, in their neighborhoods, and even in their country. It's often helpful for parents to offer specific examples of what parents, teachers, police officers, and airport security managers are doing to make their world a safer place. When you try to reassure a child that she is safe, don't dismiss her fears. Don't say, "You don't have anything to worry about," or, "Why are you so worried about that?" Children can feel embarrassed or criticized when their fears are minimized.

In times of crisis, like 9/11, we have a tendency to believe that events that have a significant impact on our lives happen with greater frequency than they do. This is a good time to offer some factual information about the statistical probability of tragedy and disaster. With children under ten, stick to simple phrases, such as, "There are very few robbers. I don't know any, do you?" "This has only happened one time. It is very rare." "No one has ever been bitten by a shark swimming at this beach."

The news coverage of September 11 was filled with positive and hopeful stories that helped children recover from the tragedy. Children saw real-life heroes in action—bomb-sniffing dogs, firefighters, and police officers. They saw lots of community events—flag-waving ceremonies of support and solidarity. The researchers at Sesame Workshop believe that all these positive images, along with an outpouring of support from the mental health community, and the efforts of their parents, helped children to recover from the events of September 11. The researchers contrasted this with the tragic events at Columbine, which had a profound and lingering effect on children's fears. The deadly shooting rampage by two high-school students that left fourteen children and one adult dead sent a message to children everywhere: You are not safe at school. Dr. Pruett explains: "Columbine horrified adults but attacked kids." The only healing that took place after Columbine, notes Royer, was in Littleton, Colorado. Around the country, children saw none of that. What they saw were the scenes of devastation repeated over and over again on TV and the visible effects of increased security—guards, metal detectors, cameras—at their schools. (I'll discuss Columbine in more detail in the chapter on school shootings.)

GIVE CHILDREN A SENSE OF CONTROL

One of the things that build resilience in children (and help people recover from a traumatic event) is giving them a sense of control over their environment. Responding passively to a danger of any sort can make a person feel overwhelmed. Remember all the acts of kindness we witnessed after the terrorist attacks— people bringing food to fire stations, people lining up in long lines to donate blood, people giving to families in need. It made us feel better to *do* something. Children benefit from that experience as well. Offer children things they can do to help: write letters to soldiers during a war, raise money for victims of a terrorist attack with a bake sale. Positive and active ways of coping can help children master their fear and anxiety.

About a year after September 11, a mother in New York City noticed her eight-year-old daughter was having trouble sleeping. She'd also noticed a piece of paper lying on her bedside table for a few weeks. One day she took a look. It was a letter: *Dear President Bush, When will the terrorist attacks stop? Could it happen again? Could it happen to my parents? Are you and Mrs. Bush scared? I am.* "I was so surprised, I didn't realize she was still thinking about the terrorist attacks," said her mother. "We'd stopped talking about it. I thought she was done. But you don't realize how often it comes up. I just wasn't paying attention." The mother asked her daughter if she'd like to mail the letter to the president and she did. She began sleeping better right away. The president sent a response: *Thank you for your letter. I appreciate hearing your thoughts. I want you to know that our government is doing all that is possible to make our nation safe. The war is about your future and the future of this country. . . . Mrs. Bush joins me in sending our wishes. God Bless you, and God Bless this country. Sincerely, George W. Bush.* "She obviously got huge comfort from that letter. She asked me to frame it, and it now sits by her bed."

GIVE CHILDREN SOMETHING TO DO—BUILD A SENSE OF MASTERY

An essential part of recovering from a traumatic event is the development of new skills or recovering old ones. Help children find things they can do to encourage a sense of mastery. An activity that builds knowledge can ease a child's fear. For example, during the war one New York City private school held an Iraq forum, sort of an Iraq 101. As Arlene Joy Gibson, head of school at the Spence School in Manhattan, explains, "The girls learned who the tribes were, where the mountain ranges are, how did we get here. We even had a guest from the United Nations come in to talk to them. As they learned some basic information about the country, you could feel the temperature go down."

Another example comes from New York's Chinatown, where the local community was devastated physically and financially by the loss of business downtown. It was the last place to be cleaned up after the attacks. The parents of kids there faced serious financial problems as well. One of the schools in the area decided to create an oral history of the event and its impact on the area. The children interviewed parents, friends, small business owners, and others in the community to create a video. The children felt enormous pride in their accomplishment. They had created a beautiful, lasting product they could share with others.

It gave them a sense of mastery and competency. They had acquired new skills and knowledge about the world they lived in.

Chris Walker, a Vietnam veteran who volunteers for the Boys and Girls Club in Augusta, Georgia, created a computer club called "Club Tech" for children aged seven though eighteen. One day a seven-year-old boy, a regular at the center, seemed upset and not quite himself. Walker asked him how he was doing, and the boy said, "My dad's leaving for Iraq. I'm really sad, and scared he's not coming back." Walker talked to him about his own experiences in Vietnam, and said, "Your Dad will come back. Look at me, I did." One of the older kids heard this exchange. The teenager was working on a digital video project and was still searching for a subject. When he heard the boy's story, he had one. The older kids made a short digital film about the effects of war on the children of soldiers. The younger kids (seven- to ten-year-olds) got involved, too, making video clips they could download onto the computer. The older teens interviewed their subjects, asking such questions as: "How do you feel about your mom or dad being in the war?" The video begins with a shot of a child crying as a father walks away and ends with a father's return. The kids had "written" a happy ending. As we've seen, writing happy endings to stories is extremely common in children old enough to put words to pictures or, in this case, words to video. It allows them to control the outcome. (You'll see younger children do this too.) The children building block towers and knocking them down then played firefighter and "rescued" people from the building. Just having a place like the computer club helps children in "normal" times and in stressful ones. They can learn new skills and pursue a passion. They have a built-in community of peers with similar interests, and adults who will listen and help. Like the children in China-town, they are proud of their creation. As the seven-year-old boy told Walker: "This video makes me feel better."

These are just three examples out of thousands of ways that parents, teachers, and community members can help children to feel in control of their world, to develop new skills and a sense of mastery. You can do it in smaller ways as well. What are your children good at? Drawing? "Fixing" things? Telling stories? Help them discover a talent. Practice it, and help them to build on that strength. Remind them of it frequently. It is a building block of self-esteem that can help a child in times of stress or fear.

Fear is a signal in the presence of danger—real or perceived. It is a critical guide through the minefields of life. Parents need to recognize and understand both the typical fears of childhood and the unique and occasionally extreme fears of their children. We need to respond to all those fears with respect (and teach our children to do the same). And when we get the sense that some-thing just "isn't right," it's important that we go to a pediatrician or mental health professional for some advice.

Crises like 9/11 or major events such as the war with Iraq get our attention. They frighten and worry us, so we assume they frighten and worry our children. As a result we pay more atten-tion to them. We are more alert to signs of stress. We focus on their emotional well-being. We're just more tuned in to their needs. It turns out parents need to do more of this in our every-day lives. After 9/11, we gathered together as a nation, shared our grief, and vowed it would never happen again. But "chil-dren's daily fears are often not acknowledged and they may not be getting the support they want and need," says Pruett. "What is critical now is understanding how best to respond to children and how to serve their needs through any challenge that might face them now and in the future."

In other words, we need to take the bullies as seriously as we take the bin Ladens, and work as hard to understand life's emotional bumps and bruises as we do to understand life's larger crises. In many ways, they are just as important to our children. Therefore, it's just as important for us to help them cope.

Managing Your Own Fears, and Helping Your Children Manage Theirs

A MOTHER and her fourteen-year-old daughter were driving on the freeway and heard an Amber Alert—a news bulletin about a missing child—on the radio. The daughter said, "Mom, this all scares me so much." Amber Alerts are used to inform the public that a child is missing, and to encourage people to report to the police any information that might lead to the child's rescue. The unintended consequence of this new national law is that it can scare both parents and children. To a child it can serve as yet another reminder that the world is a scary place.

It's tough for anyone who hears one of these alerts not to become anxious for the safety of the missing child, and not to feel anxious about the safety of their own children. When parents are confronted by their child's fear—as this mother was—it's hard not to say, "Don't be scared," and then leave the subject alone. Parents often get so rattled by their children's emotions, in this case fear, that they lose their center, says Denny Luria, a clinical psychologist based in Los Angeles. "Parents respond to the effect—the anxiety—and can't deal with their child's feelings. They get so concerned with their child's anxiety that this leads them astray."

It's a natural urge to comfort a child, notes David Walsh, and a natural urge to avoid feelings that are uncomfortable. "I think the urge to comfort is something that's pretty strong—kind of a parental gene. I think it's an extension of the urge to protect. And, also, some of it is selfish. What I mean by that is certain emotions are kind of messy. So fear and things like that are messy. And I think there's a certain part of all of us that would just as soon not deal with the messiness. So when we say to our kids, 'How are you?' What we really want to hear is, 'Everything's fine, Mom,' or, 'Everything's fine, Dad.' Because if the answer is not that, and if I'm trying to be a good parent, I have a certain responsibility to respond. So I think if we're really honest with ourselves, some of it involves a little bit of selfishness. That we want our kids to be okay so that we can sit down and relax and read the paper."

A child may express powerful emotions in a variety of ways: A three-year-old may cling to your leg in fear; a six-year-old may ask, "Are the bombs going to come here?"; a nine-year-old may voice her fear in a more adult way, saying, "I'm scared." It may be a natural parental desire to comfort and protect a child, but **it is not your job as a parent to make your child's feelings go away. It is your job to acknowledge her feelings and to help her understand and manage them.**

All the experts I interviewed agreed the first thing that you as a parent must do before you answer a child's question is to make sure your own emotions are in check. In our conversations with our children there are plenty of emotional triggers. Sometimes children's feelings unsettle their parents. And sometimes the event itself—for example, terrorist attacks, kidnapping, or war—is frightening. Many times we are scared too. Whatever the source, children can read their parents' emotions very well. Children have exceptional emotional radar—they pick up adult emotions well before they understand them. And children respond to the feelings they sense in their parents. "If they see Mom scared to death," says Patricia Owen, "they're going to be scared to death too, and that's not good." After all, we're trying to make them feel better, not scare them more.

James Garbarino, author of *Parents Under Siege,* says parents should recognize that the emotional message they convey with their tone and body language is more important than any specific words they use. He studied the effects of parents' emotions on a child's reaction with the following experiment. The National Committee to Prevent Child Abuse created a special edition of the comic *Spider-Man* to educate children about child abuse. Elementary-school children were given the comic to read, and then asked: How did you feel after you read it? Garbarino assumed that if parents read the comic book first it would reduce the children's anxiety. The children would know they had a place to go to talk about their questions and concerns. He found exactly the opposite was true. Overall, more than half the children said they felt anxious reading it. The story was after all about child abuse. But if parents had read the comic book before they gave it to their child, more kids were likely to say they felt anxious or afraid. Garbarino says, "I think this happened because parents who read this comic book were made very anxious by the content—the physical abuse of children. So when they approached the child about the book, their anxiety level was coming through. Rather than reassuring the child, the child says, " 'Wow this is so scary it upsets my parents.' "

In order to truly comfort a child, parents must approach troubling or frightening issues calmly, with a sense of confidence and reassurance. Experts all agree on this point. "Parents need to monitor their own reaction," says Robin Goodman. "It's okay to be sad but not to be weepy and stay in the house all day because you are so anxious. Having kids experience your emotions is one thing, having them privy to the full intensity of them is not good. Kids model what their parents do, and look to them to be reassuring."

In much the same way that kids see everything, they typically hear everything too. Frances Stott, dean of academic programs at the Erikson Institute in Chicago, an independent school of higher education specializing in child development, tells the story of a four-year-old child who a few months after September 11 began wetting her bed. The child's mother, a teacher in Chicago, believed she had protected her daughter from the coverage of the terrorist attacks. So she just could not figure out why the child was regressing by wetting her bed. Dr. Stott and the mother talked at length, exploring what was going on in the life of that child. Finally they came upon a clue. The child's grandmother had been visiting. She was extremely worried about the anthrax that had been sent through the mail. The grandmother and the child's mother had been talking about it a lot. The grandmother was so anxious she'd even been wearing latex gloves and microwaving the mail. Stott believes this child probably overheard their conversations, saw the rubber gloves, and sensed the grandmother's fear, and all of it made her feel very anxious.

Robert Evans says that it's quite common for children to react to what they overhear adults talking about, and that children will pick up on what the adults are concerned about. Experts suggest saving any heated, tense, or anxious adult discussions for when the kids are not around. Then too, parents can themselves inadvertently create fear in their children. "There are some kids that show a reaction and it turns out that what they are reacting to is not just the event somehow, but to a parent who has been constantly harping on it, worrying about it, asking them about it, peppering them with questions, whatever. You can get someone nervous if you keep after them enough," explains Evans.

How you react to children's concerns can be significantly more important and memorable to children than what you actually say. But, of course, there is no formula for precisely how to do this, just as there are no "right answers" to children's questions. But here are some of the ways the experts I spoke to suggest parents manage their own fears before they have a conversation with their child.

EXPLORE YOUR OWN FEARS FIRST

If your child raises a subject that triggers your own fear, anxiety, or anger, it helps to acknowledge and understand your emotions on the subject. "If an adult is really frightened about the war, for example," says Luria, "then they have to sit down, breathe deeply, and maybe talk with a friend about their own fears. 'I'm scared, it makes me anxious, it reminds me of . . . ' Before they help their own child, I think they have to be aware that they're scared, and if they are aware, that can be calming too. I think that means for a parent to really stop and acknowledge their own feelings about a subject before they discuss it with a child, because you can't get rid of your fears. If you're scared of it, you're scared of it." Beth Garcia, who runs the Manhattan Kids Club, a private preschool and daycare for children under five, says she's noticed that parents in her New York City community have become more aware of the importance of managing their own emotions since the terrorist attacks of September 11. "That's one of the biggest changes in parenting in the last year and a half—everyone is really beginning to realize that they need to take care of themselves and deal with their own feelings." She keeps a contact list of therapists and counselors handy for parents who call and request some extra help. "With all that's going on you really have to work as a community and deal with what we're feeling as adults for our kids," she adds.

One mother, the wife of a firefighter who died at the World Trade Center on 9/11, brought her four children into NYU Child Development Center for a psychological assessment. The doctors told her they had "moderate stress levels" that were not uncommon in children who had experienced the kind of tragic loss they had, and suggested they would benefit from therapy. But she felt the experience would be too foreign, and too stressful for them. She decided the best thing she could do for her children would be to go into therapy herself. "I truly believe a well-adjusted parent sends a message to children," she says. "I can handle the issues and questions as they come. And if I don't know the answers I have someone I can ask."

EXPRESS AND ACKNOWLEDGE YOUR FEARS

While it's important for a parent to be clear about his own fears, it is not necessary to deny those feelings. In fact, it can be helpful for children who are learning to respond to their own feelings to hear parents express how they feel. When you do this, use a confident, even tone of voice. "It is important to describe your emotions in a measured way, and using a calm and soothing tone. Saying, 'I'm so freaked out by this I can hardly stand it,' and getting anxious yourself isn't helpful. Instead, say in a calm, even voice, 'The war scares me too, but this is how I think about it. It's not going to come close, it's not going to enter our home. It's not going to be in our neighborhood,'" says Luria. In addition to expressing your own emotions, when you tell a child, "That makes me feel worried/scared/angry too," it acknowledges the feelings she is having as well. And it lets her know it's okay to talk about them with you.

It often helps a child to hear some of the ways we manage those fears. You might say, "I was so upset this morning that I took a walk in the park. Seeing the green grass and the tall trees helped me to calm down," or, "When I heard the news I felt so sad that I cried and cried. But crying really made me feel better." As children get older, they need to begin to comfort themselves. When you offer suggestions, think of things that have helped them in the past. Some examples: "You look sad, would you like to sit on my lap?" or, "You look scared, would you like to draw a picture of how you feel?" Children like to come up with their own solutions. It gives them a sense of accomplishment and mastery. You might ask, "What would make you feel better?"

The experts agree that this isn't always easy to do. Stott calls it a "psychological two-step"—acknowledge your own fears, check them at the door, and then step over the threshold to help your children manage theirs. If you are having a hard time handling your own emotions, Evans suggests an honest but measured approach in which a parent might say something like, "Gee, I get a little more upset about this than I wish I did." If you just cannot manage your emotions on a particular issue, if you are in fact simply "too freaked out," Garcia advises letting someone else take over. "If Mom is feeling scared or anxious—maybe Dad should answer the question and not Mom because her feelings are too strong for her to keep contained," Garcia suggests.

YOUR FEARS ARE NOT THEIRS

Despite all the traveling I do, going through the new security checkpoints still makes me feel a bit anxious. Removing jackets, belts, and shoes, and getting "patted down" by a federal screener—it all gives me a little knot in my stomach. And I worry that it will frighten my kids. Yet my four-year-old son zips through the process with great enthusiasm, asking eagerly, "Do I have to take my shoes off, Mom?" and plunking his teddy down on the conveyor belt to be x-rayed. He's not frightened a bit. At home, he'll even pretend to be a security guard and ask me to put my arms up so he can "wand" me. An elementary-school teacher told me that older children, too, seem to be taking this in stride. She overheard some schoolgirls sharing stories from their family vacations. One girl eagerly reported details that included "and I even got body-checked at the airport." Anxiety-free, these girls were just reporting another adventure on spring break.

Kids clearly pick up on their parents' emotions, but they do not always share their fears. In the weeks preceding the war with Iraq, one seven-year-old girl had heard her parents say, "If we go to war . . ." so many times that she finally asked them to stop saying it. Her mother said, "I think I said things like, 'If we go to war, Dad won't be able to go on spring break with us.'" The little girl was not afraid of the war as an adult might be, but worried—rightly so—that her vacation might be interrupted. In countless ways, it is clear, children's fears *are* different.

Parents often make assumptions about what their children are feeling. And often, they make the wrong assumptions. For example, parents often assume—as I did with my son and traveling—that if they are worried about something, their children must be worried about it as well. But children have their own unique filters; they pay attention to what they want and hear what they want. Sometimes they get upset for a brief period of time and then they go right back to being themselves. To this day, one six-year-old boy who is fascinated with spatial relations asks when he sees a really tall building, "Is it bigger than the twin towers?"

It's easy for parents to misread their children's behavior. "Parents will often assume if they're very worried and their child doesn't seem very interested, that the kid must be hiding things—they must be burying feelings. But I think until you get more evidence, it's a mistake to imagine that. It can be true but it needn't be necessarily true," notes Robert Evans. Sometimes children are just not worried. And sometimes they take a while to work through their feelings. A teacher at Manhattan's Church Street School for Music and Art told me that one of her three-year-old students exhibited a great deal of anger after the attacks but became "tight-lipped" when asked why. Several months later, she was cleaning up an art project with the boy and on the floor there were two long strips of tape. The boy became quiet, looking at them. "They look like the World Trade Center towers," he said, asking, "Did you see it?" "Yes," she said. "I saw it on TV." "I saw it come down," he answered, creating an opportunity for discussion.

Often children will manage the impact of an extremely frightening event gradually. They will move right back into the routines that make them feel safe. By comforting themselves, in their own way, they are managing their fear. Judith Myers-Walls, a Purdue University professor and specialist in child development and family studies, says, "They may not want to engage in a conversation about it just then." Myers-Walls says that parents often misread the child's reaction, believing it's not on the child's radar screen at all.

Some children act blasé or bored with upsetting events, which can be quite puzzling or even upsetting to parents. "We saw this kind of behavior a lot during the war with Iraq," says clinical psychologist Ruth Peters. "We heard children say things like, 'Who cares about this stupid war?' and, 'Why don't we just blow them all away and get it over with?' It may be extremely upsetting for a parent who hears a child say something like that. She may wonder if her child is heartless or cruel," Peters adds. But she also says this is a "reasonable and healthy" reaction for a child. "It's a good protective reflex," she explains. "If an adult isn't protecting a child by shutting out the world of adults, they'll do it themselves" by dismissing an event as irrelevant to their daily life.

IT'S IN THE NEWS, IT'S ON YOUR MIND, SHOULD YOU BRING IT UP?

A mother of six-year-old twins in New York City had been closely following the news reports of the war with Iraq. She'd heard some "experts" on television advise parents to talk about the war with their children. So she sat down her boys and began, "Boys, I just wanted you to know some news of what's happening in the world. And I wanted you to hear it from me. Our country is at war. Now you are very safe here at home, and at school. The war is in Iraq and it's very far away." One of her boys grew silent, the other burst into tears and wailed, "Mommy why are you telling me this?" As she told me afterward, "Those experts who keep telling us we need to talk about this with our children clearly don't know what they are talking about!"

If there is a frightening event in the news, and parents believe their children will hear about it, should parents bring it up? There seems to be no "right" answer to this question. As Dr. Kyle Pruett admits, "There is no categorical, good quality advice that tells you what to do. You are a unique talking machine and your child is a unique listening machine."

Whether you bring up a frightening or troubling subject depends on many factors: your parenting style, your child's age and temperament, and the nature of the event itself. Most experts agree that if you bring up a frightening event that's in the news in the "right way" it can make children feel that there is a place to go when they have a question. Evans offers, "It's easier for me to say that the extremes are not good for kids. One extreme is that you are rubbing your kid's face in stuff that he or she is not really interested in, doesn't grasp, or doesn't care. The other extreme is in which you deny questions, shut off debate, pretend things aren't happening and ignore overtures from the kid. Anywhere in the middle I think there's room for parents to have fairly different styles about how they handle these things so it fits into the natural way the family relates and works together." Pruett says when a parent asks him whether he should "bring it up" or not he will ask the parent—what is the purpose of the discussion? "If a parent says, 'I just have this feeling, and he gets kind of quiet when this comes up,' well, that would be an indication to me that a child is ready, and does want to know about it. If a parent says, 'I believe it is my job to keep my child abreast of all important political events,' that's a different answer. The parent is saying I have an educational responsibility because I know the other kids are talking about it. I would then say to that parent, 'Well, what is it you really want your child to know? What is the best thing for your child to understand about the war in Iraq?' A parent might say, 'The United States has an obligation to keep the world safe for democracy.' When parents hear themselves say something like that out loud, they'll realize it sounds like preaching. Parents should have their own dialogue before they have these conversations with their children."

A mother of three girls, ages eight, six, and two, from California told me this story. One night a "special report" bulletin crossed the screen, followed by President Bush addressing the nation. Her oldest daughter yelled in excitement, "Mom, the president of the world, he's on TV!" After the address, in which

President Bush appeared to tell Saddam Hussein he had forty-eight hours before the United States invaded Iraq (after the first minute or two, despite their initial excitement, the girls largely ignored the rest of the speech), the mother had her first discussion with her daughters about war. She turned off the TV. She said, "There is a bad man who lives far, far away," at which point she pulled out a globe to visually show her girls just how far away Iraq is. She went on to explain, "We are very safe here. The United States is going to go help the people of Iraq." When her eight-year-old asked, "Will people die?" the mother replied, "Yes, people may die, but our country will make sure as few people die as possible." The same daughter responded, "Will the bad man die?" The mother said, "We do not want to kill the bad man, but if he continues to hurt people in his country, we may have to." She said they seemed to absorb the information calmly. During the war, however, she never let the girls watch TV and always screened the images on the front page of the newspaper. The mother said she tries to really shelter her girls, but a lot of these issues come up when children are in car pool and she felt she had to discuss the war.

Pruett explains that some events are "frightening human moments" and children benefit from talking to their parents about them. He says, "I think it is very important for adults to make the distinction that events like the war, September 11, and school shootings are in and of themselves incredibly frightening, and such an event is rendered far more frightening for the bulk of children if you do not discuss it with them. That adds mystery, and a measure of unspeakability about it. With rare exception, secrecy only serves perpetrators, not adapters, fixers, or people who are trying to cope." Obviously parents have to use judgment

about this. Pruett suggests this approach to raise one of these issues with a child, " 'You know, I have been thinking about what's
going on. It's been on my mind: soldiers, troops, and things. And
I wonder if it's been on your mind too? [Silence.] Well, if you
ever have any questions about it, I'm open to it, and there are
some things I could share with you.' You may have to do this two
or three times before a reluctant child will eventually say,
'Well . . . you know something . . .' but you have given a child
permission to come onto this sound stage with you and you can
have a dialogue and a discussion. 'You're not a bad child if you
don't have any thoughts about it. You're not a great child if
you do have thoughts about it, but it has been on my mind.' That
has the great advantage of being honest without being intrusive."

Myers-Walls adds, "If the parents don't ask about it again, it
can lead to a 'cycle of silence' " where the child believes the parents don't really want to talk about it, and the parents believe
their child isn't interested. As always, the key to understanding
a child's behavior is to ask.

For preschoolers of four and five, Goodman recommends
raising issues gently and briefly. She suggests saying something
like: "There's been a lot of stuff in the news about people fighting in other countries. I don't know if you've heard anything,
but I just wanted to let you know that everything will be fine
here, you don't have anything to worry about." She says your
child will probably say "okay" or perhaps have a question or two.
Probably by age six, she says, they will have heard about current
events, and may have a few questions.

James Garbarino believes that with elementary-school children, bringing up what he calls a "salient" event such as the terrorist attacks in New York City is a good idea. As we learned

earlier in "Fears of Childhood," children from six to twelve are more vulnerable to trauma. A mother of two boys, ages five and seven, who lives in Georgetown, noticed that her older son was much more terrified than her younger one during the twenty-two days the area was terrorized by a sniper. "My seven-year-old knew there was a guy with a gun shooting people," she said. Garbarino adds, "Very young children can be shielded from this kind of information. Elementary-school-aged children know more than their younger brothers and sisters, but they do not have the ability to protect themselves or master the information as a teenager might." He says you can look for opportunities to discuss these "salient" events in a relaxed way, at dinnertime, or when driving in the car. For example, during a car ride you might ask, "Was your teacher or were the kids in your class talking about what happened in New York?" or "What did you think about that?" Garbarino warns parents not to jump to any conclusions until they have a better picture of what the child knows and wants to know. Is she afraid? Or does she simply want more information?

Another approach Garbarino advocates: Look for clues in your child's behavior that indicate what he calls "anxiety arousal," signs that a child is troubled. He suggests commenting on a child's behavior as a way to begin a discussion: "I notice that you are locking the door to your room at night," or, "I see you have your toy soldiers lined up on your windowsill. I'm wondering what's going on?" When you get some answers, he says, you can begin to have a discussion about the event that's troubling the child and help the child to manage his feelings about it.

One of the arguments for "bringing it up" that I find most compelling comes from psychologist Michael Cohen, who also is president of the Michael Cohen Group, a research and consulting firm specializing in work with children. He believes that children—over the age of six—are hearing about big news events whether their parents know about it or not. "Parents always underestimate what kids at this age know, what they hear about, what they are exposed to," he insists. "We want our children to be more naïve. We want to keep them children as long as possible. It is a loving thing to wish for a child—the wish for a longer childhood." He says it is a natural reaction even from a savvy parent. "I do the same thing every week with my own daughter," he says. "I'm continually surprised by what she knows." If it's a big news story—like the sniper attacks in Washington, D.C., or the Elizabeth Smart case, kids who are in grade school have probably heard about it, or will soon. Parents should assume they have heard it! And if you don't set the dialogue, he argues, someone else will.

"It's a parent's responsibility to be proactive in situations that involve a danger or risk to a child," Cohen says. "You'd bring up the subject of sex or drugs, for example." The same is true for other risks to a child's safety. "These are good opportunities," he says, "to talk to children about how we prepare for things that rarely happen." Include a simple and clear safety lesson. For example, in the case of a child's abduction such as the case of Elizabeth Smart, you'd tell a child how rare this is, but also give her some simple things she can do to protect herself if a stranger approaches. (I'll provide more detailed examples of this in the Question and Answer chapters that follow.)

In the long run, Cohen believes, bringing up a scary subject will reassure a child and lower her level of anxiety. But he adds there are more good reasons to bring it up. "Each conversation is a building block, a piece of an ongoing relationship," he says. "Your child will appreciate that you brought it up, or that they felt they could come to you with anything. Children love this. They feel your love. This is an ultimate act of caring."

IS IT OKAY TO TALK ABOUT A TRAUMATIC EVENT?

Can you do harm by talking about or bringing up a frightening subject? According to Dr. Goodman, "Contrary to parents' fears, talking about violent acts will not increase a child's fear. Allowing children to keep scary feelings to themselves is more damaging than open discussion." Experts agree on this point. No matter how frightening some feelings may be, it is far more frightening for a child to feel as if no one is willing to talk about them. If they're scared themselves, children may misinterpret our silence. They may believe that we are too frightened to talk about it, or that they are silly or bad for having those fears. They may not want to upset us by bringing the subject up, as the Sesame Workshop research suggests. All of those things only serve to make a child feel more frightened and more alone.

Dr. Perry says, "Children do not benefit from 'not thinking about it' or 'putting it out of their minds.' There's no need to bring it up on your own, but if your child does bring it up, don't avoid the discussion. Listen to the child, answer questions, provide comfort and support. We often have no good verbal explanations. But listening and not avoiding or overreacting to the subject, and then comforting the child, will have a critical and long-lasting positive effect."

I'd sum up a lot of the advice on the question, "Can talking about it make it worse?" as, "Not if . . ." Most experts suggest, as Pruett does above, that when you bring it up, you should have your child's needs and concerns on your mind, and not your own.

Dealing with a child's powerful emotions may be uncomfortable, scary, or unpleasant, but it is one of the most important things we do as parents. It is important to children during times of crisis, but also important in daily life. Parents cannot assume that when adults are feeling safer, children are as well. What's become routine to adults can be very disturbing to children. Children need us to understand that, acknowledge it, and help them deal with it. But they should not have to help us sort out our emotional issues too.

So what about the mother of the fourteen-year-old daughter who said, "Mom, this all scares me so much." How did the mother respond? She said, "You know, that scares me too. But then I think well, yes—there are kidnappers around, but we're safe in our house. I am strong and can handle anyone who comes into our house and wants to hurt you." This parent did all the right things. She did not get rattled by her daughter's fear, but stayed calm. She did not dismiss her daughter's feelings by saying, "Oh, you have nothing to worry about." She spoke in a strong but calm and soothing tone. Now in this case the mother is a therapist trained to help people express their feelings. And this teenager is clearly able to express her own. But you can see from this exchange how a child might receive comfort, reassurance, and some assistance in managing her fear from just a short exchange with a calm and confident adult.

A Matter of Faith

Life is like a journey from New York to California. The difference between having a religion and being active in it or not is you can get to California with a map or without a map. But having a map makes it a lot easier because you know what to avoid and what not to.

—Reverend Monsignor Thomas J. Hartman

FAITH IS ONE of the anchors of human experience. It guides the way we live. It guides the way we parent. It guides our children's lives. And it can help us answer some of our children's toughest questions. So how do faith and religion shape the way we parent? How can they help us in challenging times?

I asked two friends and colleagues I've consulted a great deal in my career for some advice—Rabbi Marc Gellman and Reverend Monsignor Thomas J. Hartman. They work as a team called The God Squad. They host a daily television talk show that is aired in the New York metropolitan area, write a syndicated column for Tribune Media Services, have written several books, and have been frequent guests on *Good Morning America*. We were also joined by their colleague, Dr. Faroque Khan, a physician and a prayer leader at the Islamic Center of Long Island in Westbury, New York.

All three men are religious leaders, and they're also community leaders. So regardless of your personal faith or beliefs, I think you'll agree with me that they have great resources, knowledge, and experience to help today's parents shape their children's understanding of the world. In these troubling times, it is even more important for us to instill in our children not only a sense of security, but also a belief in the goodness of mankind.

So here's what my handful of experts had to say.

Q: How does faith guide us through life and its challenges?

RABBI GELLMAN: Religion teaches people hope. It teaches them lots of things but it teaches them, I think, above and beyond anything else, hope. And what is it? What kind of hope is this? Religion primarily teaches people that death is not the end of us and that after we die, God will take care of our souls one way or another. God will protect the souls of every living thing. That death is not the total final culmination of everything about us is one of the elements of hope.

The second element of hope that religion teaches is that people are basically good. Even though there's evil in the world, people are basically good. Human goodness—people helping their friends, people doing acts of sacrifice and charity, bravery, courage—all these things are very much a part of human nature. That's the part of hope I always share with people who are not religious because sometimes people who are not religious can be put off by religious professionals.

MONSIGNOR HARTMAN: What I have found is that faith teaches you that we're all sons and daughters of God. Faith encourages you to think in terms of perspective, not only as

Americans but also for instance of the Iraqi family and what they're going through. When you start doing that, you become willing to pray not only for yourself but for other people. And then your children begin to see you praying and they ask you sooner or later, "What are you praying for?" And when you teach them prayers and teach them to think of the people first in their own immediate circle and then other people, their relatives and some people that they've seen on the news, their dog, their cat, they begin to tell their story to God and rely on God and ask God for help. And then faith becomes real.

Sometimes faith makes you stop and think. We have a tendency in our lives to jump at the immediate. Somebody hits us; we want to hit him back. Some circumstance hurts us; we want to have an immediate reaction. What faith does and prayer does is make you stop, take a look at the entire perspective, and then act. It slows you down. It makes you more patient and it makes you more broad in your interpretation of your options.

Q: How does faith or religion guide us as parents?

DR. KHAN: For the Muslim, the basic understanding is that we have been placed on this earth for a predetermined period of time. The Muslim will be held accountable for all their actions in this world and we have a very strong belief in the concept of heaven and hell. So for the Muslim whatever happens in this life is really a period of trial for the eternal life. And that becomes the general background or backdrop for all the actions which a Muslim takes. All that he is involved in—whether it's a crisis or it's a happy occasion—it's basically that the Lord giveth and the Lord taketh. I'm expected to do some things based on the teachings in the Koran and traditions of the Prophet but ultimately the Creator is in charge of the total package.

MONSIGNOR HARTMAN: Faith starts out by believing in God, parents teach by their love and by their own example. You teach children from the earliest times of their lives that they are made in the image of God. You teach them that there's a light inside them called the soul, and it's connected to God. You teach them that the most important thing in their life is not their body but their soul, their spirituality, their character.

What parents do is first they absolutely love their children. Their presence assures their children that when negative things happen in life that they will care for them, that they won't abandon them. They will cure them with doctors' help. Parents should tell their children that they can turn not only to them but they can also turn to God. And sometimes when their parents aren't there they can talk to God themselves.

RABBI GELLMAN: I think the heart of the matter is that there really are just two possibilities in raising children. One is to teach them that anything that makes them happy is good. The other is to teach children that they stand before the presence of a higher power. This higher power calls them accountable and wants them to live virtuous lives and demands that they sacrifice and help people beyond themselves. It's the collapse of religion that accounts for many of the problems in the culture. Religion is the central civilizing force in society. That, and, of course, the family.

In families the fundamental point is that children need to be taught that they were put here to help others and not just themselves. Now people can get to that without religion. But they can't get to that without the values that religion has basically maintained for two thousand years. I don't care if they are formally affiliated with a religious institution, but I think it is much easier for people to come to these values when they are taught them in religion.

Q: How does religion help us answer our children's difficult questions?

DR. KHAN: Religion allows us to fall back on previous history and on previous traditions and reassure children that what they're going through others have gone through in the past. It may seem kind of overwhelming at this time. But with patience and forbearance and belief, one has a better chance of handling all these complicated issues. I face this all the time in my medical profession. A young person is dying of an illness while somebody who's ninety-plus isn't. It doesn't sound fair.

MONSIGNOR HARTMAN: In Christianity there's the notion of compassion. One of the first things that happens when a person enters a church is they see Jesus on the cross. And the teaching is that there is suffering in the world but there's something beyond the suffering. You can give meaning to suffering.

When we see Jesus on the cross and then Jesus rising just a few days later the teaching is that while we go through suffering we will be redeemed, we will be healed. But in the meantime when we see suffering, we're meant to try to lend ourselves to the curing of the suffering. Jesus, when he leads the apostles, says "I'm going to send you and as you lay your hands on others they will be healed."

RABBI GELLMAN: I call religions "wisdom traditions" because wisdom is different from intelligence. That's a key thing that children and adults need to know. There's a difference between being smart and being wise. Smart is just knowing the facts about the world and there's plenty of smart people in the world. Our schools basically teach people how to be smart and teach them the facts. However, very few institutions teach people how to be wise. The only one I know of is religion. It's the reason why every culture has religion and why it never goes away.

Now, how does religion teach people how to be wise? And what is wise? Wisdom is different from intelligence because wisdom is knowing what matters. Intelligence is knowing what is. Wisdom has moral connections to it—the whole Enron thing is all about people who are very smart but not at all wise. Religion teaches people about wisdom. These are traditions that are thousands of years old and have been teaching people wisdom for thousands of years—and they're very good at that. It's really the only place you can go if you want to be wise. It's why it's very important to me that people are religious. I know people who are atheists who are wise but it's a lot harder for them to get to that place because they never believed that there's anything beyond them. Religion teaches us that God is beyond all of us and beyond all leaders and beyond all nations.

Q: How can we as parents use faith to help a child who is afraid?

DR. KHAN: Basically the message from Islam is that we're all faced with ups and downs in life. We're all faced with temptation. And we need to stand up for what's right. In the long run, eventually the truth prevails. So in other words there is hope. There is hope and there is salvation and being good ends up eventually being rewarded. Now for a Muslim there is strong belief that you may not get all the rewards in this world. But if you hang in there, eventually on the day of judgment you'll get all the good, and be rewarded for all the good deeds you have done.

MONSIGNOR HARTMAN: Hope is the virtue that we believe that God has a plan or a purpose. We don't always see it. We don't always know it right away but we believe enough in God to believe that God's in the mix. We're going to learn something or become something or be led to a deeper understanding of the mystery of life. We will learn something from this. It's a decision to say I will trust that God will speak through this moment. I will trust that we can figure out another plan of action. I will trust that something good will come from this. Even though it may not be the good that we thought was going to come from it.

RABBI GELLMAN: We began with the idea of hope. For people who are not religious and even for those who are, hope is the key portal to enter the message of religion. I have learned that just as fear is contagious so, too, hope is contagious. And religion helps spread the contagion of hope rather than the contagion of fear.

Q: What does your faith, your religion, say about killing and/or war?

MONSIGNOR HARTMAN: Catholicism sees war as a failure of communication. When we use force instead of words we're in danger of killing each other, arming each other, disabling each other, Catholicism would lean toward a more pacifistic approach. There is justification in certain instances for war when somebody has been attacked and they're called upon to defend themselves, what is called the "just war" theory. But the attack must come first from somebody else and the response must be appropriate, with appropriate means. Not overwhelming.

DR. KHAN: There are good people and there are bad people in this world and they've always been like that. Islam permits waging a war but there are very, very strict guidelines. And it basically states that if someone oppresses you and someone doesn't allow you to practice your faith and someone kicks you out of your home, you're allowed in self-defense to gain back your rights. Islam does not permit an offensive war. It permits a defensive war. There's no such thing as a holy war. That doesn't exist in Islam. Now if you wage a war with those basic principles, there are some very fundamental guidelines. Number one, noncombatants should not be harmed, which means women, children, and elderly folks. They cannot be touched. Even to the point that if there's a fruit-bearing tree, that cannot be cut down during war. Because that would harm the community in the long run. Number two, if the opposing party seeks peace, the Koran says very clearly go out and seek peace. So yes you are permitted to fight for your rights, but if the other party is extending a hand, grab it. So these are the basic fundamentals of war in Islam.

RABBI GELLMAN: There're two great traditions that come out of organized religion. One is the idea that there is "just war"—it's okay to fight wars. The other is that it's never okay to kill anything or anyone. I think a fair reading of the New Testament would indicate that Jesus' view was religious pacifism, and it's certainly the Buddhist view. It is not the view of the church or Protestants or Catholics, who have endorsed "just war" theories for two thousand years. The basic idea I try to explain to kids is that the Ten Commandments for the New Testament has "Thou Shall Not Kill." The Jewish commandment is "Thou Shall Not Murder." The Hebrew word is the word for murder, not killing. And that is a huge and important point because if it is killing that God prohibits then war is always impossible. But if it is murder that God prohibits then killing in war and killing in self-defense is permissible.

Q: So how do you explain war to children?

RABBI GELLMAN: The first thing to explain to kids about war is that there is evil in the world. Even though people are basically good sometimes there are really, really bad people and sometimes they invade other countries and oppress their people just like the Pharaoh did in Egypt. And these people have to be overcome. Sometimes they can be overcome by talking to them but that's very rare. Mostly they have to be overcome by defeating them. And the people who defeat them are very important in our lives. They are called soldiers. And these soldiers are very brave and they keep us safe.

Q: What do you say to a child who asks if killing is bad, or why we have wars?

RABBI GELLMAN: Well, I speak in a fourth-grader's voice. I would answer it's because bad people have to be defeated. The people who defeat them in wars are good people and courageous people and they keep us safe.

MONSIGNOR HARTMAN: I would talk to a child and use examples he can understand. For instance, I would say—you know when you go to school and you have classmates and you like your classmates but it seems as though there's always one or two kids in the class that give you trouble? They get into fights and they make life miserable for other people? So that's what happens in the world. There are many countries and God loves all of the countries but sometimes the people of certain countries do things that make life difficult for other people. And they pick on others or they cause fights and consequently somebody says, well, we have to stop that because it's bad behavior.

Q: What if a child asks why God creates bad guys?

RABBI GELLMAN: This is a very hard topic. I've had a lot of success talking to children about it but it's a very philosophical point. God doesn't create bad people. The point is that God has given us free will and that means we can choose good or bad. And if we choose bad that bad can be very bad and it can hurt millions of people. That's how great evil comes into the world—with bad choices.

DR. KHAN: I suppose it basically comes down to free will. People have been given free choice and free will. As a Muslim, I've been given a choice to do good or to do bad. And I've been told that the one who gave you that choice is going to judge you eventually. So I'm constantly living with that thing hanging on my head. If I decide, yes I can do this, I can do that, then I'm accountable for it. It comes back to the basic Islamic teaching that this life is a trial. It's a test. So to have a test you must have choices and you must have options. And a human being is given the options of doing good or doing evil. I don't think people are made evil. People make choices which are not right choices. I have patients who get addicted to alcohol or get addicted to drugs. They're not bad people. They just made bad choices and must face the consequences.

MONSIGNOR HARTMAN: When God makes a child, God loves that child and will always love the child. And God gives the child a very special gift. It's the gift of choice. We have a choice of doing good things or we have a choice of doing bad things. The reason why there are bad people in the world is some people have forgotten to make good choices. They start doing bad things and it's like going out into the winter cold. They want to go outside without a coat on and it's okay for a couple minutes. But if they stay out there for a while they're going to get numb and they won't be able to feel anymore. Well, the same thing with people who do evil. When somebody asks you to do something evil like curse or fight or hurt other people, if you do it once, and then you do it again and again and again, after a while you become like that person out in the cold weather for an extended period of time. You become numb to it. You think you have a right to do it. And so the person who is watching you has to say to you that's inappropriate. That's the wrong thing to do. So God doesn't create people bad. People make bad choices.

Q: And what about "bad things" that happen, such as natural disasters?

RABBI GELLMAN: Earthquakes and hurricanes are natural evil, and the point about those are that they aren't really evil. There's nothing evil about a big wind. It's only something bad if people put their houses where the big winds go or if they put their houses where the big floods go or where the earthquakes come. But there's nothing basically bad about an avalanche or an earthquake. They're just the way the earth breathes and without it breathing we wouldn't have oxygen and we wouldn't have all the things that enable us to live. That's how I explain natural evil.

Q: What can you say to a child who's afraid that bad guys are coming here, and asks is it going to happen again, am I safe?

MONSIGNOR HARTMAN: It's very important for adults to give children security, to tell them even though we can't guarantee a hundred percent that nothing bad will ever happen we have to act as though nothing bad will ever happen. We have to say to children there are certain things that adults can take care of and there are certain things that kids can take care of. You can take care of not cursing. You can take care of not stealing. You can take care of not fighting with other children. But the idea that somebody from another nation is coming, that's the job of an adult. And the country, the president and his helpers are making sure that through the police, through other good people, that this won't happen again. They're instituting procedures, they're setting up laws, and they're making sure that anyone who thinks about doing something bad will not do it.

Q: After the terrorist attacks and after something like a Columbine, what if children ask why people want to hurt us?

RABBI GELLMAN: Some people want to hurt us because they know that we are a country of freedom and they don't want their own people to get the message of freedom. And that's one reason. Another reason people hurt us is not by wars but as individuals. Maybe they're jealous or angry and they can't control their anger. And their anger leads them to hurt others.

DR. KHAN: I would tell the child that what was done was wrong. There was no justification for flying machines and planes into a building where people had gone to work. Then the follow-up question is, well, why did they do it? Why did they kill themselves in the process? Our religion is very clear on this. The religion very clearly says that if you take one innocent human life, it is as if you have taken the life of humanity in total. So life is very precious in Islam. It's given by the Creator and we are expected to take care of it. So for somebody to fly a plane and kill three thousand people is murder. It's as simple as that. It's terror and it's murder. Now then the child can ask again, but why did they do that? And then we can get past the religion and try to give them a little understanding of the geopolitical situation. There are a lot of angry people in the world. There's an anger and resentment about the haves and the have-nots. Some people are living in poverty and there are all kinds of reasons why they hate us. That kind of discussion can go on. But religiously speaking, there's absolutely no justification for the kinds of acts that we have seen.

MONSIGNOR HARTMAN: Many people differ with the way we do things. Some people don't like capitalism. Some people don't like our power. Some people don't like the American way of life. And those people have all the right in the world to say that and to have a dialogue about that. That's appropriate activity. But if somebody doesn't like us and they choose to hurt us, that's an inappropriate activity. When the pope was at the United Nations in 1998, he said that the next millennium is going to be decided on how nations treat each other. It's just like a family. In a functional family, the strong nourish the weak. In a dysfunctional family, the strong take advantage of the weak. So those who have objections to our way of life have every right to criticize. They can even help us at times by critiquing us. When we get too puffy or when we get uncaring of other nations, that's good. But if they choose to terrorize us, if they choose to destroy us, that's evil.

Q: What does God say to help us when we are afraid? What do we tell our children?

MONSIGNOR HARTMAN: Whenever I was a child and feeling afraid I used to go to my mom and dad or my grandmother and tell them I was afraid. They used to listen and then they used to say it's going to be okay. We'll get through this. I'm so glad you told me you're afraid. Let's pray together or let's talk about it. They were interested in what I was going through and how I perceived it. When you have faith you feel comfortable to do that with God. You can ask God to help you. You can go to a church or you can pick out a special place in your home. A special chair or some place where you just want to feel comfortable talking to God. And you just share with God what's happening and you ask God to help you. And God will.

Religious beliefs are intensely personal. But after talking to my own version of the three wise men, I found it comforting that despite their different religions, their messages were very much the same. I hope that this message is one that you can use to help formulate your responses to your child.

PART II

Their Questions,
Your Answers

Conversational Comfort Zone

As HARD as we may try to protect them, children today have access to adult information—and lots of it. They collect news in bits and pieces. The barriers between the world of adults and the world of children are more porous than they've ever been. As a result, it has never been more important for parents to help children manage all this incoming information, and manage the often-frightening feelings that go along with it.

"Psychologically, a kid can go anywhere with a fact. You just have no idea where they are going with it," says Dr. Michael Cohen. Children relate new events, for example, to things they already know or things that are relevant in their world in ways that make perfect sense to them, but often no sense to adults. It's nearly impossible to predict how a child will process something. And parents shouldn't assume that we know.

For example, Cohen remembers that when he was a child during the Vietnam War he heard the term "guerilla warfare" and it terrified him. He believed the Vietnamese army had trained ferocious gorillas to attack American troops. To an adult, this is cute, a play on words. But to a young child listening to war reports on the evening news, this literal interpretation makes complete sense. Cohen's story reminds us just how impossible it is to predict how a child will process the "news" he gathers. It is also a reminder that it is our job as parents to figure it out—to discover the unique ways our own children understand their world.

In this chapter, we'll learn some ways to create what I call a "conversational comfort zone" where both children and parents feel at home. It's a place where children can get help understanding the information they've collected; it's a place where they can ask questions and sort out their feelings; and it's a place where they can get answers and reassurance. It's also a place where children can feel listened to. For parents who know that listening is the most important thing a parent can do for their child, it's a place where they can do this carefully.

It's not always easy to unravel the mystery of what's going on in a child's mind. So we'll learn how trained professionals who talk to children every day do it. I'll show you what you can do to help figure out just what your child knows, and needs to know, what she's thinking and feeling about all kinds of issues, particularly the troubling ones.

THE LONG AND WINDING ROAD FROM THE HEADLINES TO THE PLAYGROUND

Diane Levin, a professor of education at Purdue University, shares the following conversation she heard in a New York City classroom of four- to six-year-olds. She included it in her book, *Teaching Young Children in Violent Times: Building a Peaceable Classroom,* and says the conversation is loaded with specific techniques adults can use to help children deal with disturbing issues. It was August 2002 and a few days beforehand, a New York City police officer had shot and killed a man armed with what turned out to be a toy gun.

The conversation began when a child said: "You can only play with water guns—not toy guns—because a robber could go into the toy store with a real gun . . ." A very clear bit of advice in the mind of that preschool child, but a very puzzling statement to an adult. As the rest of this scene plays out, you'll see the children were thinking a lot about toys. But as this teacher discovered through some careful questioning, there was a lot more on the children's minds:

JOSEPH: You can only play with water guns—not toy guns— because a robber could go into the toy store with a real gun and put it with the toy guns. You would take it thinking it was a toy gun and you could shoot someone with it.

TEACHER: So you think a robber could go in a toy store?

HENRY [turning to teacher]: Are there really robbers?

TEACHER: What have you heard about robbers?

MARGARET: They take things like money and jewelry.

RANDY: Is that what a robber does?

KEVIN: They have guns. They can *really* shoot them.

MARGY: Only real guns can shoot, not toy guns. That's why there are water guns for children. I can have them.

TEACHER: Yes. Grownups work hard to make sure that children don't get hurt by real guns or by robbers.

RANDY [hesitantly]: When someone takes a child is that a robber?

TEACHER: Taking a child? Have you heard something about that?

MARGARET: Yes. A robber is anyone who takes anything, even children.

TEACHER: There aren't a lot of robbers—hardly any. I've never known a robber!

BRAD [excitedly]: I didn't either. Neither did my mother or father!

SHIRLEY: Mine didn't either!

KEVIN: Well if you saw a robber you'd know anyway. You can always recognize a robber!

TEACHER: So you would know if you saw a robber? Tell us how you know a robber.

KEVIN: He wears a black shirt and black pants, and black shoes and a black hat.

TEACHER: So you would know if you saw a robber because he wore black? [A couple of children say yes.]

TEACHER: So you know a lot about robbers. How did you learn about them?

KEVIN: At school. We saw a movie. On TV. It told us about robbers.

RANDY: I had a dream about a robber that had a toy gun that looked like a real gun—no one knew it was pretend.

TEACHER: So you had a dream about a toy gun? When was that?

RANDY: Last night. I slept with my mom!

TEACHER: Dreams can be pretty scary. It sounds like sleeping with your mom helped. That's good you had something you could do to make it less scary.

MARGARET: That really happened, you know. He got shot with a real gun. [Other children nod in agreement.]

JOSEPH: Yeah. He had a toy gun but it looked real.

BRAD: No. Robbers don't have toy guns!!

KEVIN: Yes he did!!!!

TEACHER: So you heard something in the news about someone—a robber—that got hurt with a real gun or a toy gun?

JOSEPH: No. He got hurt with a toy gun. That's why you can't play with toy guns. Only water guns.

HENRY [proudly]: I have a water gun. It shoots really far. My mom got it for me.

TEACHER: So some of you can play with water guns, not toy guns, because your moms and dads think they're safer. Guns can be scary and hurt people. Grownups work hard to make sure guns can't hurt you. [Several children nod.]

By listening closely, and asking the right kinds of questions, Levin says, the teacher in this situation learned how these children were processing a nugget of adult information. She realized that the children had heard the news story that had been widely covered earlier that week. The children had then created their own, unique meaning of that news story, as children typically do, and were sharing it with the other children. In a way the children were playing their own version of telephone—passing on what had now become a jumbled version of the news story.

WHAT'S REALLY GOING ON IN THIS CONVERSATION

The teacher in this classroom was puzzled by the association the boy made between toy guns and real guns, and she began to explore the issue. As Levin explains in her book and discussed with me, here's what the teacher does:

- **Listens very carefully** and repeats back the children's observations. This is called active listening. When the teachers asks questions like, "So you think a robber could go into a toy store?" and, "So you would know if you saw a robber because he wore black?" it lets the children know she is interested in what they have to say and that this is a comfortable place to have this conversation.
- **Asks thoughtful questions** to find out more about what the children know. This often yields clues about what they

want to know. The teacher asks questions like: "What have you heard about robbers?" and, "So you would know if you saw a robber? Tell us how?" This is perhaps the most valuable technique a parent can learn! **It is very important to really understand the meaning a child is creating in her own mind before you answer her question.** Using questions like some of the ones this teacher used can help get to the heart of the matter.

- **Reassures children** that they are safe by saying, "Grownups work hard to make sure that children don't get hurt." To provide perspective, she also offers some concrete evidence that robbers are very unusual as she says, "There aren't a lot of robbers—hardly any. I've never known a robber!" She does this a few times. Also, notice that she does not rush in to "teach" or correct misinformation. She lets the children talk and she listens.

- **Acknowledges feelings** when she discovers them. By saying, "Dreams can be pretty scary," she allows the children to express their emotions, and lets them know it is okay to talk about them. She also acknowledges how helpful it is to find things to do when you are frightened when she says, "It sounds like sleeping with your mom helped. That's good you had something you could do to make it less scary."

This skillful teacher successfully connected her responses not to the *stated* comments of these children, but to the *meaning* those comments had for them. When we are faced with a troubling, or even simply puzzling question from a child, parents need to do the same thing. If we hear a comment that doesn't make sense, or watch a game that just doesn't feel right, we need to connect what we observe to the meaning it has for the child. In all of our significant conversations with our children, we need to constantly make connections to their world—to try to see the world through their eyes.

Here are some of the things parents can do to connect with the world of children—to create a conversational comfort zone—when they are faced with tough questions. You can find out what your children know, what they need to know, and ways to answer their questions that provide comfort and reassurance.

THE ART OF THE QUESTION

The critical first step in responding to a child's question or concern is to determine what he actually knows. In journalism 101, this is called the 5 Ws: Who, What, When, Where, Why. You want to give the child an opportunity to tell you his own story. There are certain kinds of questions that will usually get the ball rolling for you—questions that will discourage the one-word answers most parents encounter, such as, "How was school today?" "Fine." Here are a few ways to phrase questions that will open up a conversation rather than close it down.

- "Tell me about . . ."

This usually elicits more of a response than "Are you . . . ?" For example, "Tell me about how you are feeling," rather than, "Are you sad?"

- **"What do you know about that?"**
- **"What have you heard?"**
- **"Where did you hear that?"**

These types of questions are often more effective than asking "Who told you that?" which implies that somehow the child shouldn't know about it, or should not bring it up.

- **"What do you know about that?"** usually encourages a child to share what he knows. **"I've been hearing a lot about that too,"** **"What have you heard?"** or **"That's a good question. What do you know about it?"** are alternatives for slightly older school-age children. Such questions acknowledge that they are out in the world learning about things, and that they might know a few things that you don't.

- **"What do you think about that?"**

Children usually feel good about themselves when you ask them **"What do you think?"** If "What do you think about that?" feels a bit intimidating for your child, a less direct approach might work better, such as, **"What are your friends saying about that?"** or, **"What do your friends know about this?"** or, **"What are your friends thinking about it?"** A child might find it a bit safer to talk about what a friend is saying. After that you can try a more gentle, **"And what do you think?"**

This is not an interrogation but a chat between you and your child. As we learned in the chapter titled "Managing Your Own Fears," the tone you use when speaking to children is extremely important. As always, when you have these conversations, try to use a calm and soothing voice. Getting physically close to a child can also encourage him to talk and make it easier for you to listen. You can kneel in front of him, sit alongside him, or sit him on your lap. Your physical closeness will make him feel safe and comfortable. You'll be able to hear him better, and to observe his behavior.

Another way to encourage an easy dialogue is to play with your child while you're chatting. Sit on the floor with some building blocks, or toss a ball outside.

Once you've begun to reveal what's going on in the child's mind by getting him to tell you what he is thinking and feeling, then you have some real data to work with as you answer a question or clear up misinformation.

SILENCE REALLY IS GOLDEN

Listen to what your child has to say, but don't jump into the void when she reaches the end of a sentence. That silence can be a good thing. It may encourage your child to say more. It will also give you a chance to observe her behavior and read the nonverbal cues. You know what your child does when she's anxious. Look for those signs. Does she twirl her hair around her index finger? Does she chew on her cuticles? Avoid eye contact? Curl her feet inward? Tune out? Ask lots of questions? For example, my son is terribly afraid of the characters at Disneyland. So a few days before we go he'll pepper me with questions. "Donald Duck really isn't going to come near me, right? He'll just wave at me, right? And you'll just put up your hand and tell him no not here, right?"

Now, finally, after holding your tongue, you can begin to talk. Here's some of what you'll want to accomplish when you do.

ACKNOWLEDGE FEELINGS

Now that you have a pretty good sense of what she is feeling, you can acknowledge her emotions. You can say things like, "I can see how you would be frightened by that," or, "You know, sometimes that scares me too," or, "Yes, that is pretty frightening."

David Walsh suggests sending up what he calls "trial balloons." Walsh says to summarize what a child has already told you, and without assuming you are correct, repeat it back to her. Follow that summary by asking: "Have I got this right?" or, "Is that what's going on for you?" For example, "Let me see if I've got this right, you think the terrorists might do something like this again, and crash a plane into another high-rise building, and that frightens you, so you don't want me to go to work today? Did I get that right?" A child may say, "Yes, that's right." Then you can continue. If he says no then you'll ask him some more questions to "get it right." Walsh says parents shouldn't feel as if they have to get it right immediately. Children recognize and appreciate your efforts to listen and understand. Those trial balloons, he believes, make the child feel the parent is really interested and working hard to understand her feelings.

It's important to avoid saying things like, "Oh, you don't have to worry about that," or, "Don't be scared. It's okay." These dismiss the importance of a child's feelings and can make him feel criticized or foolish. As Robin Goodman points out, "The minute you say, 'Oh, don't worry,' a child thinks: 'I shouldn't have told you that I'm worried,' or, 'I guess it's bad to worry,' or, 'I guess I'm pretty stupid to have worried.'" So then what does that do to help your child's anxiety? Not a thing. What you can do to help a child is offer him ways to understand and deal with his feelings. And you can begin by providing some clear and simple information.

TELL CHILDREN WHAT THEY NEED TO KNOW

The standard advice is to correct misinformation, and offer age appropriate answers. How do you know what age appropriate answers are? A few ways. First of all, a point I keep coming back to repeatedly is that you know your child better than anyone else. You know his temperament, how his mind works, and how he handles new information and new feelings. Usually once you've figured out how much he knows, you'll have a very good sense of what you need to say to comfort and reassure him.

Another useful guideline when giving information to children—especially young children under six or so: Less is more. Every expert I talked to used the same story to illustrate this point. Clearly it's a classic in child development circles. A boy asks his mom, "Where did I come from?" The parent takes a deep breath and launches into an explanation of the birds and the bees. At the end of the story, the boy looks puzzled and responds, "Well Johnny says he came from Minnesota. Where did I come from?"

Conversations may be brief and may contain only small amounts of information, but they are part of a process. Jama Laurent, a Los Angeles–based clinical psychologist who frequently works with children, says, "You just keep with it until you know they've had enough." I think it's a bit like feeding babies. If you are paying attention while you are feeding them, you'll notice when they go from ravenously devouring the bottle or cereal to a more curious sampling of it. They'll smile up at you, chew on the spoon a bit, until finally clenching their mouths shut or pushing the bottle away. You can read children's nonverbal cues the same way. Are they looking calm or anxious? Unsettled or satisfied? Have they lost interest and gone halfway down the hall when you're midsentence? That's probably a good sign that they've had enough. You may have heard this analogy before, but I think it's a good one. But, of course, reading your child's cues in real life is never quite that simple.

A story of a mother's compassionate and heroic efforts to help her child begin to grieve is seared into my memory forever. Tara Stackpole is the mother of five children, ages eight through twenty. Her husband, Captain Timothy Stackpole, was a New York City firefighter, a legendary character of superhuman strength and bravery. In 1998 he was severely burned in a fire, and he spent two and a half years recovering, fiercely determined to return to the job. He made it back to active duty at Division 11 in downtown Brooklyn just days before the terrorist attacks at the World Trade Center. On September 11, he was in the South Tower when it collapsed. Tara Stackpole shared this story, an example of how she's long used that same analogy to answer the questions of her children.

"Somebody told me when my first child was born that the best thing you could do was 'spoon feed your child information.' And that's how I handle small questions and staggering disasters. I always try to determine how much they can handle, and spoon feed them just that much. It's always worked for me until 9/11.

"When I saw those images on television," Tara recalls, "I just knew there was no way he survived. I still had hope, but I am practical and that took over. I didn't say anything to my children. I knew they had to come to this in their own way, and I couldn't suffocate their hope.

"You have to understand the culture of the firefighters that my children grew up in. We all believe that the firefighters can handle anything. That they can survive in impossible situations. And their dad certainly had done that before.

"A few days after the towers fell, my ten-year-old finally asked, 'Mom, how many days can a person survive without food or water?' I knew how hard it was for him to ask me that question. But I also knew what he was thinking. 'Dad is alive somewhere in a basement under those buildings.' So I took a 'spoon feeding approach' and began, 'You know it is very unlikely that anyone is still alive.' At that point, I knew I was going to have to be honest. I got a few sentences into the conversation and he put his hands over his ears, and screamed, 'Mom, stop! You told me too much.' I was trying so hard to be careful, and I messed up. For ages, I was worried that my son would be screwed up."

This is as traumatic a conversation as any parent will ever face. This mother made a judgment call based on her instinct and her knowledge of her child. Did she get it wrong? Maybe. Or maybe there was just no easier way to have this extremely painful discussion.

Tara knew how hard it was for her little boy to come to her with that question and she did something just as hard—she told the truth, as gently as she could.

OFFER CONCRETE INFORMATION

Children under ten think concretely, so offer simple, factual information. When they are frightened or anxious, for example, you can respond with lots of specific details about how hard adults are working to keep them safe. For example, you might say, "Mom and Dad always lock the doors at night," or "The U.S. military has a missile defense system that can detect a bomb heading toward this country and keep it from reaching us. That's just one of the ways in which the government helps keep this country safe."

On her website, wendymogel.com, psychologist Wendy Mogel says: "Yes, we psychologists will tell you that some of their questions are really a cover for anxiety. We'll tell you that, rather than answering the questions directly, your children will profit more if you can unearth or pinpoint their underlying fears. But sometimes a cigar is a cigar. Or worthy curiosity about science or theology. So if your child asks why the World Trade Center towers fell when the planes crashed into them, find out. Okay, I'll tell you this one. According to Hyman Brown, the engineer who oversaw the construction, it was the 24,000 gallons of burning aviation fuel that turned the steel into a soft noodle, not the impact of the crash. The towers melted. If they ask about search-and-rescue techniques, military operations or life after death, or if all Arabs hate Jews, more often than not respond by saying that's a good question. If you don't know the facts, get the encyclopedia or browse the Web together. Excavate the facts or the philosophy the children are seeking." This is one of the places where knowing your child and how he processes new information is extremely important. If your child likes lots of details, offer as many as you can think of. If your child is better with one chunk of information to mull over, and gets overwhelmed by too many bits of information, even reassuring information, then back off. You can always have the conversation again after she's thought about it a bit.

When people get frightened, they tend to lose their sense of perspective. It goes right out the window. It happens with adults and it happens with kids. Because so many of the things we are afraid of are extremely rare (terrorist attacks, kidnappings, and so on), it's both honest and effective to point that out. Again, you'll have to use concrete analogies to illustrate the point because children at these ages cannot always grasp the idea of probability. For example, a child in Minneapolis might be worried that the sniper attacks in Washington, or the war in Iraq, would come to his home. To help the child understand the improbability of that happening, a parent could pull out a map or a globe to show the child where he is situated and where the event that is scaring him is happening. If you are using a map, you can illustrate with thumbtacks how far away you are from the event. I'll give you some more examples of how this is done in the chapters that follow.

OFFER WAYS TO COPE WITH THEIR FEELINGS

One of the most helpful things you can do for children who are frightened or anxious is to help them find ways to cope with those emotions and find ways to create a sense of control over their environment.

With younger children who are less verbal, have them draw pictures. Put out some crayons and paper and draw with your child. When they are able to write, children will often add captions to their drawings. Older children sometimes will draw pictures and write stories with happy endings to go along with them. It reassures them that all will be well.

You also can help children come up with something they can do to make themselves feel better. Some classic examples: turning on a night-light or lining up stuffed animals to act as guardians against scary nighttime invaders. It's important to ask a child: "What can we do to help you feel better? More safe? Less frightened?" Typically a child will enjoy coming up with a solution of his own. It gives him a feeling of accomplishment and this active response will make him feel better.

If a child is frightened of crimes or disasters, create an "emergency" plan with her. For example:

- If a bad guy comes into my room, I'll grab my bear and run down the hall to Mom and Dad's room to escape.
- Dad and I will pack an emergency kit with water, snacks, and a flashlight. We'll leave it in the hall closet in case we need it. If we do, I'll go get it right away.
- If I hear more about a terrorist attack coming I'll tell Mom to make sure she knows all about it.

Children, like many adults, do better if they have a plan. It anchors their anxiety. After September 11, homes and office buildings throughout the country conducted fire drills and drew up emergency evacuation plans, which helped many people feel more secure because they knew there was a plan. Children also do better if they have a script they can follow. You can rehearse the lines with them over and over. These steps make them feel more secure, and in a real emergency they will follow the plan.

BE PREPARED TO DO THIS ALL AGAIN . . . AND AGAIN

This is a process, not a one-shot deal. If your child is really bothered by something, you'll have these conversations again. And even if you have put one issue to rest, you can be certain there will be others.

THE CHAPTERS AHEAD

In the chapters that follow, I have collected real questions from children and, using the advice from experts, have suggested some ways you can answer these questions. The questions and answers are in dialogue form. We engaged in role-playing exercises. I played the role of the child asking the questions. The experts answered, as a parent would. They look like scripts, but they are simply illustrations of how you can put to use some of the suggestions I've offered. They'll show you how, when you craft an answer to a child's question, you can use some of the advice I've just taken you through. They'll help you find out what your children know and what they need to know, acknowledge their feelings, offer age appropriate information, and provide ways they can cope with their emotions.

The next chapters cover some of the issues that often come up for our children in these troubling times: media scares, kidnapping, school shootings, emergency preparedness, war, terrorism. I've also included a chapter with some of the questions children typically ask about death. I've put the questions the youngest children (ages two to five) ask first, and follow them with the questions older children (ages six to nine) might typically have.

What I've discovered as I've collected questions from kids and gone to experts for answers is that despite the variety of ways a child can formulate a question, the underlying issues are remarkably similar. You'll see in each of the following chapters some common themes emerge. "Am I safe?" "Are Mom and Dad going to be here to take care of me?" So while you'll want to choose your words carefully, what's really important to your children is the message of comfort, safety, and reassurance. They may not remember the words you use, but they will remember you made them feel secure, less frightened, and more in control of their emotions.

They'll remember that they can come to you with any kind of question, and all sorts of thoughts and feelings. And when you think about it, that really is the best thing you can do.

What follows are suggestions and tips I've gathered from people who are trained to talk to children. I offer them to you to use in your own way to fit the specific needs of your children. I hope these tools become building blocks of a lifetime of conversations.

Death

FEARS OF DEATH OR DYING

DEATH is a difficult, weighty, and delicate topic. It is one of the essential mysteries of human life. Adults wrestle with the issue of death, and in their own ways, so do our children. There are volumes of academic research and scores of books for parents on death and bereavement. While in our brief discussion I can't provide an intricate examination of the subject, I am including this chapter because questions about death and fears about death or the death of a parent underlie many of our children's questions about other frightening events.

The questions that follow are questions children typically ask as they begin to understand death. For the purposes of this book, I am not exploring issues of profound grief and bereavement and therefore have not included the kinds of questions children who have suffered a significant loss, such as the loss of a parent, would ask.

My grandmother passed away recently. And among my initial thoughts were how was my mother going to cope with her grief, and how was I going to tell my son? Because my grandmother lived far away, he wasn't terribly close to her. Her death, as sad as it was for me, was not as significant for him. But really, I had no idea how he would react. I knew that I had to allow him to see that I was sad, but not be so upset that it would scare him. So that night at dinner I said:

"I got some news today that made me very sad. I want to tell you about it. Grandma died today."

"Did you cry?" he asked.

"Yes I did. I was very sad when I heard the news."

My husband added, "Grandparents are very special people to us." My son quickly cut him off.

"Where did she go?"

"You mean, like heaven?"

"No," he said. "Where did she die?"

"Oh, a hospital."

"How did she get there? An ambulance with the lights on?"

"No, a car."

"Who took her?"

"Your uncle did."

"Was she sitting up?"

"Yes, she died at the hospital later that night."

I was a bit startled by the line of questioning but he seemed completely satisfied by the answers.

Children start to understand death at around the age of four, says Kathleen McCartney, a developmental psychologist and professor of education at the Harvard Graduate School of Education. "They are usually exposed to it through the death of a grandparent or great-grandparent, or a pet." It comes up in the stories they read and the movies they see: *Babar, Bambi, The Lion King.* Frequently four-year-olds will become preoccupied with the topic, as mine was. You'll hear them say things like, "I can't talk, I'm dead," or, "Let's play dead," as if they enjoy using the word. At this age they begin to understand that things that die will not come back. In child development lingo this is a cognitive skill called reversibility.

Reverend Margaret Graham of St. John's Church in Georgetown, Washington, D.C., says children's understanding of death progresses as they age. "At the ages of three through six, children's sense of death is finite," she says. One day at her parish school, the children arrived to news their pet bunny had died. "They knew the word 'death.' They knew the bunny was 'dead,' but they still expected the bunny to return the next day. Their sense of immortality is not well framed, but they can use the word."

By ages six through nine, they are more curious, and ask more questions like, "Why did the bunny die?" But they still don't completely understand the passage of time. "Forever doesn't translate well for kids," she adds.

By age ten, a child usually understands the concept of death—its universality, irreversibility, and the loss of ability and function. Robin Goodman says, "By the age of ten or so a child will understand that death happens to everybody, it can happen at any time, that a dead person does not live or breathe, or come back to life as we know it. All of those things are part of what we know as the physical components of death." Of course, a child's developing religious or spiritual beliefs shape her idea of what happens after death.

Death is a significant and complex concept for a child to come to terms with. This is one where they really need our help. There is no reason why you should "wing it" when you talk to your kids about death. Talk to your spouse about it. Get a book on the subject. Talk to your priest, minister, rabbi, or monk.

WHEN A CHILD ASKS QUESTIONS ABOUT DEATH

Every expert I spoke to about answering children's questions about death said each parent must construct an answer based on his or her beliefs. But as you'll see below, experts emphasized the importance of the concept of an afterlife for children. Until the age of ten or so, children think very concretely. "They need to know where we go when we die," says Ruth Peters. "They want to know there's a heaven. They want to know they'll see their grandma there, or their pet that has died. It is a compassionate and very helpful response for kids to hear." A mother of two boys ages four and six said her children's grandmother, "their favorite person on earth," created a magical image of where she would go when she passed away: She told them when they are older, she will live on a "different planet" and they'll have a spaceship to visit her.

As I watch my own son at the most elementary stages of an effort to create his own meaning for the concept of death, it strikes me that it's an almost instinctive response from a child to fill in an answer, and to do it in a way that may make sense only to him. Here's an exchange we had recently:

"Martin Luther King is in our knees," my son said to me on Martin Luther King Day.

"Martin Luther King is in your knees, really?"

"Yes, he died but he's in our knees and our muscles."

That day at school, the children learned about Martin Luther King, Jr. The teacher said something along the lines of, "Although Martin Luther King is dead, he is still in our hearts, and in our minds." Somehow muscles got included in that list. It's a perfect example of how children take a bit of adult information (he died, but we still remember him) and attach it to a reference point they know (he's with us—in our knees). And it illustrates how comforting it is for a child to know that someone who dies goes somewhere.

When a child asks questions about death, what she often fears is that she may die or that a parent may die. One of the things that frighten young children the most is the notion that a parent might die, and no one will be there to take care of them. Harold Koplewicz explains: "Because children are so egocentric at this age, if they hear about someone dying they want to be reassured that their world is safe, that Mommy and Daddy are going to be safe, and that Mommy and Daddy will be there to protect them as well."

In some of these answers you'll discover a "white lie" or two. Many experts believe that it is of primary importance to reassure young children, under the age of seven, that their parents will always be there to care for them. The idea that "there are no guarantees" is too complex and too frightening for a young child. A parent can introduce the idea that "most of the time" people live until they are very old when a child is seven or eight years old.

Here are some questions children frequently ask as they process the idea of death, and some suggestions from experts about how you might answer them.

• • •

QUESTIONS

"Am I going to die? Are you going to die?"
"Why do we die?"
"When will I die?"

"Where do you go when you die?"
"What does dying feel like?"
"Does it hurt to die?"

Child: Am I going to die? Are you going to die?

Parent: Yes, *we* will all die. But not right now. Moms and Dads live a very long time so they can take care of their kids. By the time we are ready to die we have lived a very long life.

Child: Why do we die?

Parent: All things die. We are born, we live, and we die. Just like flowers, only we live for a very long time.

Child: When will I die?

Parent: No one knows when anyone is going to die. But most people live until they are very old. Moms and Dads live for a very long time because they need to take care of their children until they are old enough to take care of themselves. That's why we are here to take care of you.

For very young children of three, four, and five it is important to address a common underlying fear that they will be left alone, and Mom or Dad won't be there to take care of them. Most experts agree that for children of this age a "white lie" ("Moms and Dads live a long time so they can take care of their kids," or, "You die when you are older after you are married and have children of your own") is—as Dr. Peters puts it—"in everyone's best interest." When a child is a bit older it's time for a parent to introduce the notion that *most* of the time we die when we're old, but that's not a guarantee. When is it time to intro-duce that idea? That depends upon your child. Peters suggests using the "Santa Claus test"—if your child still believes in Santa Claus or the Easter Bunny you can wait a bit. Once they stop believing, it's time to let them know that no one really knows when we'll die. It's important to reassure them honestly, without promising, "We'll be here *forever*," but to reassure them that you will be there to take care of them.

Child: Where do you go when you die?

Parent: You go to heaven. (You go to a better place, a happier place, a beautiful place.)

Or for an older child:

P: Where do you think we go? What do you think happens when we die?

Let them explore what they think about this issue with you. Again, Peters says that, in her experience, older children (ages seven to nine) will usually answer at great length.

Again, everyone I spoke to agreed that the answer to this question is completely dependent on your own beliefs about the afterlife, but children under the age of ten think concretely and really need to have a picture of where you go when you die. Even if we don't know the answer, a child needs to know that when we die we go somewhere. In this case, if we don't fill in some of the blanks for them, and fill them in with a comforting thought, they may create frightening images in their head. A child might imagine we lurk around as ghosts do, or end up in a dark place all alone. Neither imaginary scenario provides much comfort. With children over the age of seven or so, encourage them to explore the issue as in the question above. They will begin to formulate their own ideas about an afterlife in a way that is meaningful and comforting to them.

Child: What does dying feel like?

Parent: I don't know. What do you think it feels like?

C: I think it feels like sleep.

P: Maybe it does. That's a nice feeling, right?

C: Yes.

P: What else do you think it might feel like?

Child: Does it hurt to die?

Parent: We can do lots of things to make people comfortable when they are dying. We have lots of medicine that people can take so that it doesn't hurt. Doctors watch very closely to make sure it doesn't hurt. We can make sure people who are dying are not alone and have someone there who will take care of them.

Again, this is one where you fill in with your own belief. But it is always okay to say, "I don't know." And then follow that by asking, "What do you think?" When a child asks, "What does it feel like?" she usually has some ideas of her own. It's important to find out what they are. Robin Goodman, who has been working with families affected by clinical illness and bereavement for twenty years, says that research with adults suggest that when they are dying, people wonder if they will be in pain, and if they will be alone. And they are comforted by reassurance that they will not suffer and will not be alone. She believes that children worry about the same things. Parents can offer children ways that doctors and other people will help a dying person to be comfortable, cared for, and not alone. For a child who does not seem to be worried about being in pain or being alone, it is helpful to allow her to explore her thoughts with you. It's comforting for a child to know she can express her thoughts, and even try out some hypothesis (it feels like sleeping) on a mysterious subject with you.

It is very hard to know what to say when a child asks about death. We don't know ourselves what some of the answers to their questions are. But it is extremely comforting for children to know that a person who has died has "somewhere" to go. Many parents will turn to their religious beliefs for guidance. Others will look for inspiration in other places. I'd like to share the following story about a search for words to offer solace to children facing the loss of a parent from a conversation I had a year ago.

In September 2002, while anchoring CNN's *Pinnacle,* I profiled former New York City mayor Rudy Giuliani. He was truly a courageous leader during a time of unprecedented crisis, and a source of great comfort to many. In many ways he acted just like a good parent should, working through his emotions—his staggering grief—in private. He told me he cried when he was alone with his feelings. In public, however, he expressed his sadness with great strength and eloquence. Searching for words to comfort others, he drew on his memory of a dear friend, the husband of Giuliani's longtime assistant, fire department captain Terry Hatton, who was killed that day:

I thought of Captain Terry Hatton. His wife discovered she was going to have a baby after we found out that Terry was lost at the World Trade Center. And I thought to myself, well this baby has as a daddy a man who won nineteen medals in twenty-one years—I used to feel like I was giving Terry Hatton a medal every day! He rescued people from fires, from the tops of buildings. He went into under-ground, collapsed situations and pulled people out, and he was a very responsible and careful person. He was a great commander who cared for his men. Just think of it—what this child will inherit and what will be inside this child. Thinking about that helped me convey that same message to children who lost their mothers and fathers on 9/11.

When addressing many of these children at the countless me-morials he attended during the weeks and months following 9/11, Mayor Giuliani would offer these words of comfort to the children of the men and women killed in the attacks: "You didn't lose your dad, he's right inside. He's right there inside you, because he helped to make you. You're—him, and your mom. And all of the wonderful things you hear about your dad, all those things that people tell you, all of that is inside of you, too, and no one can take that away from you. Absolutely no one. Death can't take your dad away from you."

I can't imagine a more comforting thought for a child expe-riencing the loss of a parent. Whether a lost loved one is in our "knees" or our hearts, our children will receive solace from knowing that they are still with us somehow.

Kidnapping

Stories of kidnapping scare the heck out of parents, and they often frighten our kids. During the summer of 2002, it felt as if you could not turn on the TV or radio without hearing news of a child's abduction.

On June 5, 2002, a fourteen-year-old girl was taken from her bedroom by a man who police believed cut through the screen door of her home in Salt Lake City, Utah. The girl's younger sister, then nine, watched it happen. The local police, helped by volunteers, searched for the missing girl for months. For the first few weeks after the abduction, the story dominated the news. Elizabeth Smart became a household name. Nine months later, shortly after Smart's parents, helped by a clue provided by their younger daughter, released a sketch of the family's handyman, Elizabeth Smart was found alive and returned to her parents.

During that summer, two other kidnapping cases received significant attention—the abduction and murders of seven-year-old Danielle van Dam of San Diego and five-year-old Samantha Runnion of Orange County, California. It felt as if we were experiencing a wave of kidnappings.

Meanwhile that summer, a little-known emergency response

tool used in just a handful of states also received widespread attention: the Amber Alert, which was created in 1996 in honor of a young girl named Amber, who was abducted while riding her bicycle in Arlington, Texas. It is an early warning system that is used by the media to alert the public that a child is missing and to encourage individuals to report any information that may help the search to the local police. According to the National Center for Missing and Exploited Children, the murder of a child who is abducted is a "rare event," but "74 percent of children who are murdered are dead within three hours of abduction." Amber Alerts are meant to get the word out, in an effort to find an abducted child within those crucial first few hours. You'll hear Amber Alerts on the radio, see them on television newscasts and on highway signs. The alerts prompted such a tremendous response from the public that politicians took notice and as a result of a new law, we now have in place a national network of Amber Plans across the United States.

When I asked psychologist Robert Evans about "the rash of kidnappings" that summer, he quickly reminded me that in a nation of 240 million people, three or four instances, however horrible, were not an epidemic. And statistically, that's accurate. According to the United States Department of Justice, 58,200 children are abducted by nonfamily members each year; 115 children are the victims of the most serious, most long-term abductions (stereotypical kidnappings), of which 56 percent are recovered alive and 40 percent are killed; 203,900 children are the victims of family abduction, which is the far more common scenario. (According to the Department of Justice, a family abduction occurs when a member of the child's family, or someone acting on behalf of a family member, takes or fails to return a child in violation of a custody order, or other legitimate custodial rights.)

The stories of kidnapping are scary, that's true. But the extensive media coverage they attract amplifies the threat exponentially. Yes, we know bad things can happen. A child can be kidnapped. But it is extremely rare. This sounds like the kind of answer you'd probably give to a child, as you'll see in the dialogues below. But parents need to repeat this mantra to themselves over and over. This is our fear, a fear disproportionately greater than the actual threat and one we don't want to pass along to our children. We need to use all that information about the rarity of child abductions by a stranger to ease our own anxiety before we talk to our children about kidnapping.

WHEN A CHILD HAS QUESTIONS ABOUT KIDNAPPING

The subject of kidnapping comes up in vague ways for children as young as three or four with fears that a "bad guy" will "take" them. Recently I saw some five-year-olds play an elaborate "game of kidnapping." They set up a bunch of large cubes as "beds" and the leader of the game was assigning a child to each bed. She said: "Sometimes a bad guy comes to take you out of your bed." I was a bit alarmed when I heard this. I asked her, "What happens when the bad guy comes?" She said, "Oh, I just run into my mommy's bed and I am okay." I assumed that these children had heard something about the Elizabeth Smart abduction. That may have been the case, but I've learned that children under the age of six tend to fear "bad guys." The precise definitions of "robbers," "kidnappers," or "terrorists" are not clear in their minds. (Nor should they be.) But the fear that a bad guy will snatch them and take them away is a typical developmental fear at this age. Barbara Gardiner, a clinical psychologist and author of several parenting guides for dealing with children's strong emotions, explains, "One of the natural coping mechanisms of children is acting out their fears. Just because they are playing this game does not necessarily mean this is eating away at them, it is most often a way for them to master their fears. Children look for mastery over scary things. Those games should not be stopped. But what should be of interest is the outcome. If the outcome of the game has the child kidnapped, that's worrisome, but if a kid ends up in her mommy's bed— that's the most natural thing in the world. It demonstrates that kids are figuring out things in their own heads."

If your child is in elementary school, a few years older than those preschoolers, she's probably heard about Elizabeth Smart. As we learned, children have great filters. They will tune out a great deal, but they tend to tune in to stories that involve children. And the visual elements of these stories have enormous emotional impact on adults and children alike. We see the raw anguish of the child's parents, crying and pleading for her return. We see pictures of the child, and are reminded of just how young and vulnerable our own children are. And we see them over and over again.

You can respond more effectively to a child's questions about kidnapping if you know the basis of the child's underlying fear. If your child heard about a recent child abduction, it is important to respond with some clear detail about the facts of that particular case. If you do not, her imagination or information from another child will fill in the details instead. Your child's re-action to seeing one of these stories on the news or hearing it on the radio will—as with all of these subjects—vary a great deal based on the child's personality and temperament and your family history. If your child is a very fearful child, and some children by their very nature are, you have to spend more time repeating your core messages, as I'll detail below: "You are safe. And this is very rare."

This is an important time to reinforce safety messages. You can use his question about kidnapping as an opportunity to talk to your child about preparing for dangerous things that happen—but reiterate that they happen *very rarely*. You can compare them to fire drills—something even preschoolers do in school—an exercise you do in case you have to respond to a fire. It's not likely to happen, but if it does you will be prepared.

• • •

QUESTIONS

"Mommy, can I sleep your bed?"
"Could a kidnapper come into my room?"
"What if a bad guy comes to school to get me?"

Child: Mommy, can I sleep in your bed?

Parent: Sure. What's the matter? Do you want to tell me now? Or do you want to go to sleep and we'll talk about it in the morning? (Note: If you get lucky here and your child wants to go to sleep, remember to ask in the morning.)

C: I'm afraid to sleep in my bed.

P: Come sit in my lap. You're afraid to sleep in your own bed? What are you thinking about?

C: A bad man's coming to get me. He's coming to take me.

P: A bad man is coming to get you? How would he get in here?

C: Through the door.

P: We have a heavy door with strong locks. No one could get through it. You are very safe in your room. And if you feel scared you can always call me or come get me.

What parent hasn't had a child come into his or her bed at night? "If they are really frightened, the sensory experience of a warm cuddle and the feeling of being protected will reduce the child's anxiety," says Marylene Cloitre, director of the Institute for Trauma and Stress at New York University's Child Study Center. "I never think that a parent should deny a child's wish for comfort. Not when they first request it." You can reassure children by letting them know they can always call you or come get you. Let them know you are there to keep them safe. When they are calm, they'll listen better to your words of reassurance. ("The heavy door will keep out the bad man.") Later, with a bit of education, as you'll see in the question and answer below, you can help them face their fears. Don't force a child to confront her fear by sending her back to her room alone, at least not at first. When she is calm—a few minutes later or the next day—you can arm her with some knowledge that will help her manage those fears herself. No one is recommending that your child be allowed into your bed every night, but when a child is truly frightened she needs to know she has a "safe" place to go.

Child: Could a kidnapper come into my room?

Parent: Well let's think about that. How would a kidnapper get in? Could a kidnapper come into your room?

C: He'd come in through the window.

P: The window? We live on the twentieth floor. I don't think anyone could come in through a window. Let's go look and see if there's a way someone could. Does it look like there's a way a person could climb up? Tomorrow morning let's go out in the daylight and look from the street to see if there's a way. Are there any other ways you're worried someone could get in?

C: The front door!

P: Well, we have the doorman out front, who only lets in people we know. At night they lock the elevator. And we have two locks on the front door. And you know, it has never happened in this building before. I think our home is really safe. I don't think someone could get into your room. What do you think?

C: I guess so . . . a man can't really climb up the outside of a building, right?

P: Right, our home is really safe, there's no way anyone could get into your room, but if you are worried about this any more let me know.

The parent doesn't assume she knows why her child is afraid, and asks questions to get him to explain what he's worried about. In this case, the parent got lucky. They live in a twenty-four-hour doorman high-rise building. She could offer a few key details—the doorman, the locked elevator, the height of their floor—and offer to look outside the next day, which gives the child another chance to reassure himself with more information. If you don't live in a high-rise and do live in a house with screen doors, walk your child around the house—show him the lock on the doors, the bright light outside the doors—anything you can do to reinforce your message that your child will be safe at home.

Child: What if a bad guy comes to school to get me?

Parent: What do you know about that? Are your friends talking about it?

C: Yes, they took that girl. And everyone was looking for her.

P: Do you think that could happen to you?

C: Yeah, sure.

P: Well, I can understand how you might be worried about something like that. But there are lots of people at school who work very hard to keep all the students safe. There's a guard at the front door. There are security cameras over every door, and they watch them in the office. The principal has very clear rules for what teachers and students should do if there's a stranger in the buildings. The teachers would not allow a stranger in your classroom. The other kids would yell and scream if they saw something bad happening to one of their friends. [Provide lots of details. Pause to see how your child is reacting. Is he calm or agitated? Is the information making sense to him? How is he doing with it?] Let's make a plan . . . let's talk about what you would do if someone tried to take you from your school. How do you think that could happen?

C: A guy could grab me on the sidewalk out front.

P: So let's make a plan so that if that ever happens you'll be ready. What would you say? What would you do?

C: I'd scream and yell.

P: That's a good idea. What else?

C: I'd call for the teacher. Hang on to the fence really tight . . .

P: Okay, so let's go over this, and practice a bit . . .

This is a variation on the bad-guy-coming-to-get-me question that a child of seven, eight, or nine might ask. They may have heard an Amber Alert. Or they may have heard about the Elizabeth Smart kidnapping, or her return. What this parent has done first is to discover what the child thinks might happen, and what bits of information he might be piecing together. The parent acknowledges the child's feelings by saying, "Gee, I can see how you'd be worried" or by asking, "Does that worry you? Does it make you scared?" This answer provides lots of details about all the people who are working very hard to keep school a safe place, many of which the child has probably not considered before. It gets the child involved in creating a plan of action that he can use in an emergency, and that will help him to manage his fear. It's important for children to create a script that they can follow in what they perceive to be a dangerous situation. For a younger child, perhaps the plan is, "If a bad man comes to get me in my bed, I call out for Mom, and then jump up and run to her room." Go over it a few times. The knowledge that they have a plan that they have created with your assistance helps to anchor their anxiety.

DON'T TALK TO STRANGERS

I was sitting with a group of mothers after our children's music class. The group of moms who'd been talking anxiously about the Elizabeth Smart case and the "rash" of recent kidnappings thought this group setting would provide a good opportunity to teach these kids—a group of four- and five-year-olds—about strangers. I realized I hadn't even raised the subject with my son. "Uh-oh," I thought, "I'm behind the eight ball again." The group asked one of the fathers to give "the talk" to lend the topic some seriousness. I was a bit uncomfortable because I wasn't entirely sure just what he would say. But I didn't want to neglect an important lesson in safety. "Does everybody know," the dad began, "what a stranger is?" The five-year-olds jumped in quickly. "Someone you don't know." They clearly "knew." But the littler ones, the four-year-olds, squirmed and looked nervous or bored. This subject was definitely over their heads. Soon they detected the eagerness of the older ones to demonstrate their knowledge. And by the time the dad was winding up with, "So what do you say when a stranger approaches?" all of them were loudly shouting, "NO!" The four-year-olds looked puzzled, and the five-year-olds had mastered the simple instructions, to just yell "no" as loudly as you can. They practiced to reinforce the message, but the whole scene left me wondering just what we'd accomplished. How would I address the subject with my son again? What are you supposed to tell a preschooler about strangers? At what age do you start these conversations? And if your child is always with an adult in public places, as most four-, five-, and six-year-olds are, do you have these "chats" anyway?

As kids we were all taught not to talk to strangers. We're

taught never to open the front door if a strange person rings the bell, and never to get into a car with a stranger. We teach the very same thing to our kids. It's our duty as parents, right? Yes, it is our duty to teach our children the skills they need to survive in the world they live in: to identify dangerous people or situations and act to avoid them. But, is the best advice to give kids "never talk to a stranger"? According to a growing body of experts, the answer is no. The National Center for Missing and Exploited Children, for example, has this advice for parents: "Telling children to stay away from strangers is neither effective nor the best advice for many reasons. Stranger isn't a concept children easily understand. Instead your child should be taught to look out for threatening behavior and situations."

So what is the best way to teach your child to identify threatening situations? Still searching for answers, I turned to Gavin de Becker, security expert and bestselling author of *Protecting the Gift: Keeping Children and Teenagers Safe (and Parents Sane)*. De Becker believes teaching kids not to talk to strangers is ineffective at best, and at worst, in his words, "destructive." His advice to today's parents? Don't raise another generation of fearful kids. De Becker says there are better ways to teach your child to navigate the world she lives in. Here's some of what he has to say:

DE BECKER: I found in writing *Protecting the Gift* that kidnapping by strangers was the number-one parental fear and, of course, I wanted to find out if it was the number-one parental risk. In fact, it's nowhere near that on the list. Kidnapping by strangers is so rare, in fact, in the United States, that a child is more likely to die of a heart attack than to be kidnapped by a stranger, and is fifteen times more likely to be shot. And obviously we never think about our kids having heart attacks, so that's an indication of how remote a risk it actually is.

Q: What do you advise parents to tell their children to keep them safe?

DE BECKER: I do have two rules.

One of them is something you can teach a child easily: "If you are ever separated from your parents, go to a woman." This rule is very simple. Very clear. Here's why: The odds of *selecting* someone who turns out to be your victimizer are outrageously low. And if you select someone who's a woman, the odds go into the zero category. A woman is also more likely than a man to stay with the child until the situation is entirely resolved. Why else does it make sense to say, "Go to a woman?" Well, we tend to say, "Go to the manager." But what is the manager? Where is the manager? A child won't know. And I particularly oppose saying, "Look for a policeman if you're lost." That's outrageous—kids don't know the difference between a policeman and a security guard. They can't tell, from three and a half feet high, who's who. And there never is a policeman. You'll never find one! But children will always know to go to a woman. What you don't want a child to do if he is separated in public is to wait for someone to choose him. Almost anyone the child chooses is better than someone who chooses the child. The likelihood of happening to encounter the one in five million predators—who would victimize a stranger in a public place who happens to be in the same mall—is so remote that my purpose is to give a child something they can actually accomplish.

The second rule is to tell your child: "I will never send anyone for you (at school, at the park, wherever) without telling you first, ever. No one will come to pick you up without your knowing ahead of time."

These two rules resolve, in large measure, the kidnapping fear. They also open parents' eyes to the myth that when their child doesn't speak to strangers, he is relatively safe. Because it's not a stranger who is going to abduct a child—it's the guy you've seen in the park before who's now looking for a puppy, it's your mom's friend who "told me to come over and give you a hand with this"—victimizers use very clever ploys.

Q: We were all taught as kids, "Don't talk to strangers." Why shouldn't we tell that to our kids?

DE BECKER: Even though it is the biggest rule ever taught to us, I do not believe in telling your child, "Never talk to strangers." It's a destructive rule for a few reasons. One is that parents like it because they think, "If I just drill it into my child, he'll understand." Parents want to take some solace in believing that their child has some control over his or her own safety. But you wouldn't choose a six-year-old babysitter, and so obviously you can't rely on your own child, who isn't even reliable enough to feed the goldfish, to take any role in his or her own safety.

The main reason why "never talk to strangers" is a problem is that if your child is with you in public, he or she will see you break that rule twenty times a day. Additionally, parents will tell their kids to "Say hello to the nice lady behind the counter," "Say hello to the person giving a sample in the grocery store," "Say hello to the postman, he has a uniform, it's okay." So we confuse our children in terms of what a stranger is, first of all. But more to the point, if they are separated from you in public, what is the one resource they will need above all others? The ability to choose a stranger and communicate with that person. And if we scare them into believing that stranger equals danger, what we are doing is turning off the intuition for where danger actually comes from—which, in the overwhelming number of cases, is not a stranger.

Also, we know in cases where children seek to apply the "don't talk to strangers" rule, they look afraid. And predators are specifically choosing children who are afraid, whose shoulders go up, who tighten up—as opposed to the children who say, "Leave me alone!"

Q: Do you teach children to shout or scream loudly if someone is trying to take them somewhere?

DE BECKER: Absolutely. All children should know that the words "don't yell" mean "yell." In movies, you see someone pulling a gun on somebody and saying, "Don't yell!" I teach kids to do just that. Because what predators are saying is: "If you yell, it hurts me and it helps you."

Q: Is there a dialogue that you can suggest that parents have with their children about safety?

DE BECKER: I like to use the example of a woman cited in one of my books. She has a strategy with her young son: If they are out and he wants a frozen yogurt, she says, "Great, you find somebody to ask where the frozen yogurt place is." She stands back a little bit and he walks up and chooses a stranger and asks, "Where is the frozen yogurt place," or whatever it is. Then he comes back and she talks to him about it a bit: "Did you feel comfortable with that person? Did that person feel comfortable with you? Did that person like you?" What's happening here is that the child is learning to develop his or her own intuition about human encounters. He's learning to understand what makes him uncomfortable, and learning to perceive when other people are uncomfortable. That kind of child, who has a strong ability to communicate with strangers, doesn't appeal to victimizers, because victimizers are looking for the child who's afraid.

Q: What else should parents tell their children?

DE BECKER: Does your child know to resist being taken somewhere? That he or she is allowed to hit, punch, scream, yell, do anything not to be dragged off somewhere? Being allowed to hit an adult is a very important component. Does your child know that it's all right to fully resist an adult? The old saying, "Respect your elders"? It's absolutely destructive—which elders? Respect everybody who's older than you? Guess what that means? Everyone on the planet earth is older than a child. And so, "respect your elders" needs to be balanced with the idea that it's okay to do anything to resist being taken somewhere in public. That is a critical issue.

And when should you begin to teach your child these strategies? De Becker says he firmly believes that children under six should not be responsible for their own safety, but that you can begin to teach them these principles when you think they are ready. Instead, parents should be sending this message:

DE BECKER: Learn what it is to fear. Because the issue isn't strangers, it's strangeness. We need to help children learn *who* to choose and *how* to choose people in public to go to. This is a far greater resource than teaching them to fear strangers.

We want our children to come to us when they're frightened, upset, or anxious, just as we want them to come to us when they're proud, delighted, and enthusiastic. And we're working hard to create a place where we can discuss any subject comfortably and answer any question with confidence.

It's in just that kind of conversational comfort zone that we can teach our children how to make their way through the world outside our home—teach them *who* to choose, and *how* to choose people in public to help them.

School Shootings

It was an event that would change the way American parents and children view their schools. On April 20, 1999, two teenage boys, armed with semiautomatic guns, entered Columbine High School in Littleton, Colorado, and opened fire on their terrified classmates. When the rampage was over, twelve students, a teacher, and the shooters themselves were dead.

The teens who returned to Columbine after the shootings were deeply scarred. One teacher there at the time told me, "Kids who were sixteen or seventeen suddenly didn't want to be separated from their parents. Other kids wore running shoes to school every day that they refused to take off—in case they needed to run. Lots carried stuffed animals with them everywhere they went. And then some students tried transferring to other schools but came back because they found they needed to be around others who'd been through the same experience."

Many parents of Columbine students didn't fare much better. A freshman student at the time says, "Kids felt weird around their parents. Parents didn't know what to do." A Columbine teacher adds that, as a result, "A lot of the kids started acting out—skipping classes, drinking and doing drugs, having random sex. When asked by counselors what was going on, they said no one talked at home—that their parents were in complete denial."

"Parents lost focus in terms of their parenting skills," says Dr. Jeffrey Dolgan, head of psychology at Denver's Children's Hospital. He adds that at a time of crisis like this, "Parents have to be removed enough from their own kids to organize what their feelings and thoughts are about this, and then share them. There are a host of reactions. If the parents are afraid, then talk about that and don't cover it. If they're angry, then talk about that and don't cover it."

Unfortunately, at Columbine, that's exactly what a number of parents did: cover their feelings. In their confusion, pain, and fear they shut down. Teachers, realizing they also needed to reach out to families in order to help students heal, came up with a strategy. According to one teacher, "What we did that worked so well was to call parents—those comfortable talking to their kids as well as all of those we were aware were not comfortable—and ask them to volunteer at the school: checking kids in, sitting in on classes, monitoring the cafeteria. What happened is that those who were not comfortable talking with their own kids became comfortable—by talking to others. Volunteering at school put them in an atmosphere of 'total honesty' and that carried over to home." When the parents were in the school, they could not avoid the subject, they could not avoid being honest about it.

Sharing fears with adults seemed to have a special resonance at Columbine. "It was trial and error in the days right after the shooting," says one teacher. "The kids were feeling crazy inside themselves. All the teachers volunteered to talk to the kids all the time.

During lunch, you would go sit with them and just start a conversation. Teachers would confide in them, which really seemed to get them to open up. I remember one shared that he couldn't sleep nights and was up at all hours, watching infomercials. His basement was full of stuff he'd ordered and never opened and he was driving his wife crazy. The kids thought that was great."

Still, "total honesty"—talking about fears—doesn't work for all kids. Dr. Dolgan says, "Kids may not always be able to express with words what they've dealt with but they can through a picture and they can through music." At Columbine, "the music teachers picked groups of kids to sing on Fridays in the halls— some show tunes, some corny forties songs, as well as our new school song, 'The Columbine Song.' Music teachers are close to kids in a way many others aren't so they knew who was having a hard time. It brought kids out and gave them a mode of expression." Other kids at the school who had trouble talking found solace writing letters to the friends they'd lost—letters that they would then place on their graves.

The media coverage, the constant replay of those grisly events, retraumatized children in Columbine and frightened kids across the country. Rumors in the press swirled about possible targets, and parents were reluctant to send their children back to school. One tenth-grade teacher at a high school near Columbine said that attendance the day after the shootings was less than half—of thirty-five students, only fifteen showed up. Still another nearby high school had a SWAT team sweep lockers and classrooms for bombs immediately after the shootings and stationed parents to guard the doors.

And while Columbine was a high-school shooting, it had a deep and lasting impact on much younger children as well. A preschool teacher in Washington's Georgetown neighborhood overheard some five-year-olds talking about "kids who don't like us." When she asked, "Is there anyone you don't like?" one answered, "Yes, sometimes there are kids who do things that are not very nice. Like kids who shoot other kids." She said she actually winced in pain when she heard that. A junior-high teacher near Columbine told me that, in the months following the shootings, her sixth-graders repeatedly asked whether they should hide in their lockers if anything happened.

This single event at Columbine—the bloodiest school shooting in American history—had a dramatic impact on the way children and their parents view their world, and view the safety of their schools.

Since then "there has been a striking change in the kinds of questions about day-to-day safety" that children ask their parents, says James Garbarino. "It created an awareness of vulnerability and danger in mainstream middle-class American families that poor inner-city families have felt for a long time." It shattered for many children and their parents the illusion that school was a safe place. And every time we hear a report about a school shooting, it reminds us of how vulnerable our children are.

WHEN YOUR CHILD HAS QUESTIONS ABOUT A SCHOOL SHOOTING

When they hear about a school shooting in their neighborhood or even in a city far away, children often want to know if this could happen at "our school." "Am I safe there? How could adults have let this happen?" With these kinds of questions it helps to offer children lots of concrete ways in which adults are working to keep their world safe, and to give them a sense of how rare these shootings are.

Dolgan recommends parents assure them that "people are working to keep you as safe as humanly possible. We love you and care about you and have a lot of concern about what you are going through and it is a little scary but you have to get back to school." He says a "safety message" like this gives kids "a little go-ahead and get to it. Move ahead."

• • •

QUESTIONS

"Why do they want to hurt kids in that school?"
"Why did they let them get in that school?"
"Are they coming here?"

Child: Why do they want to hurt kids in that school?

Parent: Why do you think someone would do something like that?

C: They were really mad. They hated them.

P: Maybe. Or maybe they are just really unhappy people. And they are showing how angry they are by acting out in ways that hurt other people. How else could they have shown they were angry? What other choices could they make?

C: They could have hit a pillow.

P: That's a good idea. A good choice. What else?

In this case, a parent of a young child is taking a truly compassionate approach by characterizing the shooters as "very unhappy" people, and avoids introducing the concept of goodness or badness. Instead he uses the word "choices." Children divide the world into good guys and bad guys. For example, bad guys do things that are bad. They scare and hurt people. Believing that a bad guy is always bad is scary to a child. It reinforces the idea that the world is a dangerous place. In the mind of a child, if there are always bad guys out there, there will always need to be good guys to protect them.

The parent addresses this fear in two ways. He introduces the idea that a person chooses to act in good ways or bad ways. He is not a good person or bad person. (The parent is probably reinforcing a concept that has come up before.) The parent offers the child an opportunity to explore more positive outcomes—choose a "good" behavior instead of a "bad" one. The parent also suggests that a bad guy could choose to act in a "good" way. The idea that people aren't always bad or always good, that even bad people can make good choices in the future, is much less frightening to a child.

This is a question from a second-grader who heard about a school shooting in a nearby high school in which several students were left dead:

Child: Why did they let them get in that school?

Parent: I don't know what happened. I'm not sure how they got in. What did you hear?

C: I heard they just walked right in the front door. They just walked right through the halls.

P: Well, I don't know what that principal did at that school. But I know there are lots of people working very hard at your school to keep you safe. Your principal stands by the front door in the morning. They have a security guard at the front desk. The teachers are always watching to make sure everyone is where they are supposed to be. They'd notice a strange person in the halls. Lots of people are working hard to keep you safe at school, but what else do you think they should do?

C: Lock the front door.

P: Oh, that's a good idea. Let's find out if they do that. If they don't maybe you can write the principal a note and suggest it. Any more ideas?

Kids' questions can often sound more grown up than they are. It is important to ask lots of questions to get at what children know because they have probably acquired a fair amount of information and misinformation. (And you can bet they are talking about it among themselves.) They probably have a few misconceptions that you can clear up. It is also important to provide as much concrete information as you can about what adults are doing to make school a safe place. Ask the child to make suggestions of her own. It will give her a sense of control. Feeling powerless or helpless only heightens anxiety. It is important for children to know they can offer suggestions, but that ultimately it is the job of adults to keep them safe.

Child: Are they coming here?

Parent: No. There are lots of people working very hard to catch them, and to make sure this does not happen again. The police department has put hundreds of officers on this case, and is working hard to catch them. The people at your school are also working hard to keep you safe, too. [Go through the list above, and add any detail you can think of.]

C: Do you think they'll catch them soon?

P: I don't know, but they sure are working hard at it. If I hear anything about it I'll let you know. And if you hear anything, before me, will you let me know?

C: Sure

This is a variation of "How did that happen?" or "Can this happen at my school?" Again, the best thing a parent can do is to provide lots of details about the ways in which adults are helping to keep kids safe.

With each new school shooting, the illusion of safety in another community, and the illusion of safety in all classrooms, is shattered again. A new group of children will ask questions. A group of second-graders in Louisiana, after a school shooting that left one student dead at a neighboring high school, asked these questions as part of a homework assignment: "Will they catch him?" "I want to know why they did that. I'm scared." "Are the killers coming to my school?" While these children need to be reassured their school is safe, what we learned from Columbine is they also need a place they can go to talk.

At Columbine, for example, the school expanded its peer counseling lounge to become, according to one teacher, "a place where they have great big comfortable furniture, kids' artwork, food everywhere, and lots of dialogue," while parents banded together to rent a "space where kids could hang out, play pool, and talk if they wanted. They'd send over brownies and pizza and they did that for about a year and a half. That was really a great release." The teacher of those second-grade students in Louisiana created a place to talk, too, when she gave her students "an assignment" to write down their questions and concerns, and discussed the students' work in her class.

Our children need a place to talk at home, as well. "We didn't need a lot of questions or people telling us that what we were feeling was normal," says one Columbine student. "What we needed was for our parents to just be there, be available, and be willing to listen." And that's something every parent can do.

Media Scares

In June 2001, a shark bit off the arm of a boy swimming in the ocean in Pensacola, Florida. About a week later, a surfer a few miles away had his leg nipped by another shark. Other shark stories followed. Soon it was the media having the feeding frenzy. Even *Time* magazine labeled the summer of 2001 the "Summer of the Shark"; all this despite the reality that shark attacks are rare occurrences and were actually less frequent than the previous year. It didn't matter; by then no one was listening.

This story is one example of how the media, of which I am a part, grabs hold of a story like a dog with a bone, chews it, shakes it, turns it over, and gnaws on it some more until it has been picked clean. And only then does the dog toss it aside.

It happens with more serious news stories as well. The anthrax sent through the mail in fall 2001 ignited the fears of a public whose nerves were still raw from the devastation of September 11. Day after day, as the press trailed every particle of the weaponized anthrax, we waited for news that someone else had received a contaminated letter, or news that another victim had gotten sick or died. The chance of a tainted letter winding up in our mailbox was infinitesimal, but still, with all the media attention focused on the story it was hard not to feel as if you would be next. We became terrified that even something as innocuous as the letters in our mailbox could carry deadly germs.

The deadly sniper attacks that happened in the Washington, D.C., area during autumn 2002 became the dominant news story of the period, pushing aside stories about the U.S. war on terror. People living in the Washington, D.C., area did have genuine safety concerns during those twenty-two days when the snipers were on the loose, but the 24/7 news climate only served to heighten the sense of hysteria. "It was more of a threat than 9/11. It affected life much more," says one Georgetown area mother of two boys, ages seven and nine. "It was October—absolutely glorious fall weather—and you couldn't even go outside. It was high season for soccer and t-ball, yet all the games were canceled. And I'll never forget this image: We were driving by this big, beautiful park that abuts Reno Road, which was vulnerable to drive-by shootings. It was a sunny Saturday afternoon and normally it would be teeming with families. It was completely deserted." She says that "on the day that the high-school student was shot, they pulled kids off the playground in the middle of recess. It looked like children had become targets. After that, everything changed. The level of panic among parents was hard to disguise." "In Montgomery County alone, there were 140,000 kids locked up in their schools," adds Douglas F. Gansler, State's Attorney, Montgomery County, Maryland. "The last thing you want to do in a crisis is to change kids' routines. But that's just what they did."

In spring 2003, we had a new scare to worry about, SARS—Severe Acute Respiratory Syndrome. News reports tracked the new and deadly disease from its beginnings in China as it widened in scope, crisscrossing the globe. While the story got rel-atively little attention during the war in Iraq, once Saddam Hussein's regime was toppled SARS became front-page news. You couldn't pick up a newspaper without seeing at least one picture of people wearing surgical masks. In a cover story on SARS even *Newsweek* called this "The New Era of the Epidemic."

I first became aware of young children being alarmed about SARS through a second-grade teacher in New Orleans. During the early days of Operation Iraqi Freedom, she was alert to signs of distress and anxiety in her class about the war, but what she overheard were questions about SARS, including a debate about whether they could get the disease from playing with a toy marked "Made in China." "I was really surprised," she said. "I would have expected lots of questions about the war, but I had no idea they even knew what SARS was."

WHEN YOUR CHILD HAS A QUESTION ABOUT A MEDIA SCARE

Significant numbers of children hear about the stories that dominate the nightly news on a regular basis. They see the pictures on the front page of the newspaper, and when they are old enough they can read the headlines. And after they do, they are usually dying to talk about it. So the kids who hadn't heard it before learn about it on the playground. Parents need to remind themselves of this all the time.

"Without factual information," says Dr. Bruce Perry, "children speculate and fill in the empty spaces to create a story or an expla-nation. In most cases the child's fantasies are much more frightening and disturbing than the truth. So tell the child the truth—even when it is emotionally difficult. And if you don't know the answer yourself, tell the child. Honesty and openness will help the child develop trust." "Every day, after school, my oldest son would ask, 'Mommy, did they catch the shooter yet?'" said one D.C. area mother. "I can't tell you how hard it was to tell him one more time, 'No, not today.'" Yet that is exactly what she did.

With the vast majority of these stories, the facts are far *less* frightening than what we or our children imagine, and the threats far less grave than the round-the-clock news coverage suggests. Parents can do their children—and at times themselves—a world of good by supplying a few key details, and by putting these events into perspective.

• • •

QUESTIONS

"Is he [the sniper] still out there? What if he's near us?"

"Mom, I don't want to walk to school today, can we take the car?"

"I'm afraid of going into the ocean, are there sharks?"

"Can I get SARS?"

"Can anthrax get me?"

Child: Is he [the sniper] still out there? What if he's near us?

Parent: What are you thinking about? What have you heard?

C: They haven't caught him. I'm scared he's still out there.

P: I can see how you would feel scared. Thinking about that is pretty scary. But, you know, no one has ever done anything like this before. I've never seen anything like this happen in my life-time. I don't think Grandma or Grandpa has ever seen it hap-pen either. It is very, very rare.

C: But it keeps happening and happening . . .

P: That's true. And I know that feels really scary, but you know there are a lot of people working very hard to catch the sniper. All the police officers in the city are working on the case and the FBI has lots of detectives searching too. And people are doing many other things to keep you safe. There are more policemen on the street. We see them every day on our way to school, right?

C: Yeah.

P: And at school, you are playing inside during recess so that you are safe inside the school building. Moms and dads are com-ing inside to pick you up. Is there anything else you can think of that would help keep everyone safe?

As always, the first step is to get a handle on what your child knows, what she's heard, and what her friends are saying about it. You may be able to clear up a few misconceptions and then get a clearer sense of what she is really afraid of. Provide as many details as you can think of, ways in which adults are working to keep your child safe—remember your child thinks very con-cretely until around the age of ten. With these incidents that dominate media coverage but are really quite rare, it is impor-tant to give a child a sense of perspective.

James Garbarino suggests this powerful visual analogy to il-lustrate to a child the probability of a rare event: Get a bag of rice, pour it into a bowl, and pick up a grain. Explain, "Each of these grains of rice is a school like ours, a school filled with many children. This bowl is how many schools there are on the East Coast [pick up a single grain of rice]. The chances of there being a shooting at your school are about as big as me reaching in and picking up this exact grain of rice from this bowl."

As you'll see in the questions and answers that follow, you can get creative. You know your child and how her mind works, so you can come up with scenarios that will make sense in her world. Here are some questions that children have asked about recent news events that have troubled them:

Child: Mom, I don't want to walk to school today, can we take the car?

Parent: No, we're walking. Why do you want to take the car?

C: Can I still walk to school today? I mean there's a bad guy shooting people.

P: A bad guy out there? What have you heard about that?

C: There's a bad guy out there sniping people.

P: Oh, yes, I'd heard about a man shooting a gun, a sniper. It happened in Washington, D.C. But that's far away from here. It is safe for us to walk to school. It's very rare that something like that happens. How many kids are in your school?

C: I don't know. A lot.

P: There are four hundred. What happens if you multiply that by one hundred?

C: Forty thousand.

P: And how many cities are there in the country?

C: I don't know? One hundred?

P: Probably more, but multiply all those kids by one hundred. One in all those people, that's how rare something like this is.

This is the kind of question a seven- or eight-year-old might ask. The parent here had to do a bit of digging to get to the bottom of why her child did not want to walk to school. Next, the parent acknowledges the child's feeling and offers some perspective about the likelihood of a sniper attack in another city. Remember, when we are frightened or anxious, we tend to lose perspective. So do children.

What the parent has done here is to use some knowledge about her child—that he is very comfortable thinking mathematically. Numbers are very accessible to him. So she creates a math problem that he can figure out to illustrate the probability of getting shot by a sniper on the way to school. It's the same idea as the bowl of rice above. If your child thinks more narratively, try another approach. For example, remember the time we drove to the beach and we tried to count Day-Glo orange VW bugs on the road? Did we see one? Could we find one? No, we couldn't find one that day and we were in the car for four hours! It's possible, but not likely.

Child: I'm afraid of going into the ocean, are there sharks?

Parent: Sharks do live in the ocean. But it's very rare that they come anywhere near people swimming. It's only happened a few times in this country and it's never happened here on this beach. I've never known anyone who's been bitten by a shark. Dad doesn't either. This is a safe place to swim.

C: But there are sharks in the ocean, right?

P: Yes, there are sharks in the ocean. But they don't usually come where people are allowed to swim. People—like lifeguards—check these beaches to make sure they are safe. And I'll watch you very carefully when you're in the water. I'll go in with you if you want. You are safe swimming on this beach.

It's not uncommon for children of all ages to be afraid of swimming in the ocean. A news report about a shark attack would only fuel that fear. In the scenario above the parent stresses how rare it is for a shark to bite a swimmer and makes it clear that this beach is a safe one.

Again, the bowl of rice analogy that Garbarino uses is one way you can do this: "Each grain of rice is a beach like ours, a beach filled with many parents and children. This bowl is how many beaches there are on the East Coast. [Pick up a single grain of rice.] The chances of you getting bitten by a shark are about as big as me reaching in and picking up this exact grain of rice from this bowl."

Child: Can I get SARS?

Parent: What do you know about SARS? What have you heard?

C: You can get sick and die. People in China get it.

P: Yes, people began to get sick with SARS in China but it is very rare here. Very few people in this country have gotten it. *No one* in New Orleans has it.

Or: SARS is a virus. When germs spread, you can catch it the way you catch a cold.

C: It's like a cold?

P: Yes, but colds are very common. We get them a lot. SARS is very rare. And there are things you can do to help prevent spreading germs, right?

C: Yes, wash hands.

P: Right, or sneezing into a Kleenex.

C: Should I wear a mask?

P: No, we don't need to wear masks. The disease is very unusual in this country. There are lots of people—doctors, people in the government, who are monitoring this very closely. If there are signs that SARS is spreading in this country, they will tell us what to do to protect ourselves.

C: Can I play with toys that say Made in China?

P: Yes. Germs that land on objects like toys die quickly. Your toys have been here awhile. Germs from the place they were made would be dead by now. Let's make a plan: What should we do to stay healthy, to keep germs from spreading?

C: Wash hands, sneeze into a Kleenex.

P: Right. And I'll listen to the news. If I hear anything about SARS coming here, I'll let you know.

This is an actual question from that New Orleans class of second-graders that I mentioned above. The visuals in a story like this—people wearing masks—are powerful and strongly resonate with children. Remember that they may not necessarily be frightened, just inquisitive or confused. Children between the ages of four and nine understand germs. In precise terms, you can explain, "This is how we prevent germs from spreading." Your explanation of how germs are transmitted will register with your child, even if he doesn't always follow through. (I don't care how afraid of germs they are, it's rare to see a child voluntarily use a tissue!) You'll note that, in the answer above, the parent reminds the child of how to prevent the spread of germs and explains to the child how rare SARS is in this country. The Garbarino grain of rice analogy is once again very useful in illustrating the likelihood of a child catching SARS.

Child: Can anthrax get me?

Parent: That's a good question. What have you heard about anthrax?

C: I heard it's everywhere and it's a white powder.

P: I would be concerned if I heard that too. Anthrax is a germ that can make people very sick. It's something that's found in nature and in lots of places it doesn't hurt people. It can be made into a white powder but it's very, very rare that you would come in contact with it in this country. It has only happened a few times.

C: Where is it?

P: When we look at the information I can show you that it's only in a few places and also, there are many security measures to protect you.

Experts agree one of the first things to do is to correct misinformation and to fill in the gaps. The parent here made this a project with the child where they tracked down some of the information about anthrax, and the parent plans to show the child that anthrax is not commonplace but actually very rare. Together, they also discovered that as serious as anthrax is, it's very difficult to make and people can't just concoct it in their basements.

The dramatic elements involved in these types of stories make them irresistible to news outlets. A juicy story loaded with drama and human emotion (Shark Bites Boy!) is aired more than once and, then, in the days following, is updated and often dissected by "experts" brought in to fill time in the world of round-the-clock news. Today, even network news—often the least sensational of all the various television outlets—embraces them too. The public "demands" it, right? As the dog chases its tail, it creates a perfect storm of fear. And our children get caught in the downpour.

The round-the-clock coverage may attract viewers eager to follow the trail of the alleged killers, vicious sharks, or weaponized anthrax—but it's important to remember that frightening news stories often yield higher ratings, which bring in more advertising dollars. The media inform, but a steady media diet of terror fuels anxieties and colors our view of the world as a deadly and unpredictable place. This scares our children, and it scares us too. In times like these, we would be better served by following the advice the experts recommend for our kids: Turn the television off. Take a walk. Ride a bike. Head for the park. We need to remind our children, and ourselves, that the world is filled with more good people than bad.

In everyday life as in times of crisis, we need to put the news into perspective for our children, first by shedding our denial that they are aware of what's going on in the adult world, and then by looking at the world through their eyes and providing some concrete and simple information to fill in the gaps. If we don't their imaginations will.

Terrorism

SEPTEMBER 11, 2001, changed the world as we know it. It's become a cliché to say it, but it could not be more true. It added an element of vulnerability to our lives that has not gone away. American adults and their children face new, previously unimagined threats. We have a new government office, the Department of Homeland Security. We have scores of new procedures that improve our nation's safety. We even have a new vocabulary. There are the "9/11 widows" and "9/11 kids," children born after the attacks who will never know the fathers they lost on that day. Arlene Joy Gibson at Spence in New York City says her middle-school students call themselves the "9/11 generation."

Many times, when the world of adults invades the world of children, the images are negative, violent and scary. September 11 was certainly all that. But we also saw images of courage, pride, and valor. We heard many stories about heroes—the firefighters, police officers, and ordinary people—who reached out to a nation in need. Stories that are hopeful and illustrate all the goodness in the world really do help children cope with traumatic events like those of September 11. "We live within walking distance of two firehouses," says ABC entertainment correspondent Joel Siegel, "and a week after September 11, I took our three-year-old over to make sure everyone was still okay. I was relieved to see that they were. For my son Dylan, the week had been traumatic—he'd watched his mother crying, he'd even seen the building on fire from our apartment window. Visiting these larger-than-life guys was the treat of a lifetime and the fire guys loved it too. He got his first hook and ladder ride—his eyes were as big as saucers—and it was all he could talk about afterward. It totally changed his focus."

September 11 galvanized the mental health community as well. Its own heroes leaped into action to help adults and children cope with the trauma of this unimaginable horror. Within twenty-four hours of the attacks, the NYU Child Study Center had put information on its websites and lined up counselors for schools to use to help counsel children. The television networks used their resources to help children as well. A few news programs specifically designed to help children understand the events of September 11 aired the following weekend. As a result of these efforts, parents and teachers had tools they could use to help children work through this event, tools we continue to rely on.

Experiencing terrorism in their own backyard may be new for Americans, but around the world it's certainly not. Israel and Ireland have been shaped by it. In this book, we've been focusing on children under nine—and in their lifetime alone, we've seen dozens of terrorist acts: chemical attacks on the Japanese subways in 1995, the murder of fifty-eight tourists in Luxor, Egypt, in 1997, the 1998 bombing of Pan Am Flight 103 over Lockerbie, Scotland, and the kidnapping of an entire theater audience by Chechen rebels in 2002. In the last five years, the particularly heinous acts of Osama bin Laden and Al Queda have dominated the news, beginning with the August 1998 bombings of U.S. embassies in Kenya and Tanzania that killed more than three hundred people, the October 2000 bombing of the USS *Cole* during a refueling stop in Yemen, killing seventeen and wounding thirty-nine, the October 2002 car bomb blast of two nightclubs in Bali, responsible for the deaths of more than two hundred, and, in 2003, the bombings of an apartment building complex in Saudi Arabia. And these are just a handful.

We can expect the news to bring us a slow and steady drumbeat of continued terror from around the world—events that resonate more powerfully for a nation that's already been devastated by an act of terror close to home.

WHEN A CHILD HAS QUESTIONS ABOUT TERRORISM

For the millions of American children who saw the events of September 11, 2001, in person or on television, the emotions they expressed and the ways they expressed them are as varied as the names and faces of the children themselves. Reactions to terrorist acts, as with all traumatic events, depend on a child's age, developmental stage, and temperament. Children who lost someone close to them, or who live in the cities directly affected, will have very different reactions than will children who live elsewhere. The impact on their lives can be far more powerful and, in many cases, devastating.

Michael Cohen, a psychologist and consultant who worked with the New York City Department of Education to study the impact of September 11 on the city's public-school children in grades four through twelve says that, of the nearly one million children who were at risk for psychological problems as a result of their emotional and physical proximity to the event, a significant number experienced severe problems, exhibiting symptoms of post-traumatic stress disorder. The study also found that nearly two hundred thousand children experienced at least some symptoms of mental health disorders that would not necessarily warrant a psychiatric diagnosis, yet did impair their daily functioning. It was not uncommon for schoolchildren to experience symptoms such as increased anxiety, panic attacks, periods of agoraphobia, and problems sleeping and eating. There were thousands of stories about children who couldn't sleep alone, were afraid of taking public transportation, and didn't want to be separated from their parents.

Those signs of distress in children often lingered for months and, in some cases, remain to this day. One six-year-old boy from Washington refused for months to get on a plane to visit his grandmother in New York. In another instance, six months after the attacks, a New York City schoolteacher was driving to work and saw one of her students stopped on the side of the road, staring at the sky. When she asked what he was doing, he pointed to several helicopters hovering over the Brooklyn Bridge and said, "They're going to blow up the bridge just like they did to the twin towers." She says, "He was paralyzed with fear, unable to walk. And this was a child who had never before expressed any concerns about September 11." Long after the war in Afghanistan, a seven-year-old girl heard a news report that said "key Taliban figure arrested." She looked up and asked her mother, "You mean they got Osama bin Laden?" It was the first time she had ever mentioned him. "What a relief," she said, "now I'll sleep better!" Her mother explains she had no idea that her daughter "was that aware, much less that anxious about him."

Children's expressions of their feelings about September 11 were as varied as they were complicated. "My five-year-old, Nick, was playing with his blocks several months afterward when I realized he was 'making believe' a plane was crashing into them," says New York–based screenwriter Dave Kopp. "It opened a whole discussion about what had happened that day."

Many children outside New York—who, in some instances, only caught a brief glimpse of the terror attacks on TV—were also deeply affected. One fourth-grade teacher in Colorado reported that, the day after September 11, she asked her class of twenty-five to express what they were feeling by drawing. Each drew the towers and in every single rendering, positioned the planes about to hit the buildings. Yet not one showed the plane crashing. Like so many adults, the children just could not bear to relive—through Magic Markers and paper—the horror of the day. In Los Angles, three boys in another fourth-grade class expressed their anger by sticking thumbtacks into the class pull-down map of Pakistan. Their response? "We're mad at Osama bin Laden." In 2003 one group of second-graders in San Francisco asked their teacher, "Last year, in first grade, we hated Osama. This year, we hate Saddam. Why do we hate everyone?"

While anger may be easier to express than fear, one of the most troubling fears expressed by this "9/11 generation" may be a fear of the future. One boy at a Georgetown school located eleven blocks from the Pentagon was asked by his minister, "How do you feel about tomorrow?" "That's really scary," he replied.

When we mark the anniversary of September 11, parents can

expect new questions as children one year older begin to understand the events in a whole new way or even see them for the first time. The now-three-year-old child who was an infant in 2001 may see planes crash into buildings for the first time. A child of five, who saw the original event and simply observed the strange sight, may now ask, "Why?" A child of eight may wonder if those terrorists will do it again. In much the same way that the news coverage of September 11 provided positive images alongside the violent and horrifying ones, we can expect coverage of the anniversary to do the same. Children may see those devastating images again, but one hopes they will see some inspirational images as well—stories of communities gathering to remember the day or to express their gratitude to the rescue workers who rushed to the scene. We still live with the threat of additional terrorist attacks, and so do our children. They may wonder whether the terrorists are coming back or develop new fears about their parents' travel, as children often did right after September 11. Here are a few things to keep in mind when you answer a child's questions about the terrorist attacks:

Young children, from around three to seven, will typically ask very simple questions. A child under the age of five who sees the planes crash into the building on television has little sense of what's real and what's fantasy. As we learned in earlier chapters, they are not able to distinguish a "live" event from a replay. They blur images of news and entertainment. To them the terror attacks may resemble a fictitious action film. They do not comprehend its significance. They are aware that it is a bad event and one that upsets adults. They tend to ask simple questions, such as, "What happened?" or, "Why did it crash?" As children get older they will ask "Why" more often and they may ask it repeatedly.

A child needs reassurance that she is safe and that adults are working to keep her safe. Give the child the facts about what happened in as simple a way as possible. A child does need to know what went on, but start with a very simple answer and increase the complexity if she's not satisfied. Let a child know this is not a fear she is facing alone. Parents, families, schools, communities, and countries across the world are all facing this together. It is very important to connect a child to a broader community after a traumatic event (as it is for an adult)—to reinforce the idea that despite the sadness of this day, the world is filled with goodness. It is one of the most important things we can do to help her heal.

• • •

QUESTIONS

"Grandpa, somebody drove their plane into one of the big buildings in New York."

"What is a terrorist?"

"Why did that plane blow up?"

"Why did they crash the plane into the building?"

"Why did they want to kill people's mommies and daddies?"

"They're just really bad guys, right?"

"Is Osama bin Laden coming here?"

"Dad, why do you have to fly on an airplane?"

"What's a dirty bomb?"

"Can I seal up my room with tape in case there's an attack?"

Child: Grandpa, somebody drove their plane into one of the big buildings in New York.

Parent: I heard that, yeah . . . [Silence.]

C: Yes, they should have been more careful.

P: Yes . . .

This was an exchange that Kyle Pruett shared with me between a four-year-old girl and her grandfather. The grandfather acknowledged the child's observation. He waited for another question. She didn't have one, so wisely he left the subject alone. Pruett uses this conversation to illustrate what occurs more often—a parent will make an assumption about what the child is thinking and feeling. But the parent more often than not is wrong. Pruett explains, "If the grandfather at that point had said, 'You know honey, he did it on purpose, he was trying to blow up the building and all of the mommies and daddies and we're really angry with him and we're going to get the people who did this and make the country safe,' if he had given her far more than the recipe called for at that moment, he could have made things worse."

The adult, in this case the grandfather, was not following his own agenda, but the developmental needs of this child. There was no indication that she was scared. She was just trying to figure out how this event could have occurred, given her limited understanding of cause and effect. That's all she wanted to know about it. And she put it in a context herself that she understood—that they had an accident, that "they should have been more careful."

As you'll see with some of the questions from three-, four-, and five-year-olds, it's often best to keep your answers short if you are getting signals that the child is comfortable and satisfied with what's been said.

A four-, five-, or six-year-old:

Child: What is a terrorist?

Parent: What do you think a terrorist is?

C: A bad guy who crashes planes.

P: Yes, that did happen but only one time. A terrorist is someone who acts in ways that frighten or hurt people. But there are very few terrorists, and lots and lots of people who are good.

An eleven- to twelve-year-old:

Child: What is a terrorist?

Parent: They are people who do very bad things to frighten or scare us.

C: Why?

P: Most times it is for political reasons. Some people see violence as a solution to a problem. It often happens in other countries.

In this case, a young child of four, five, or six wonders about the new word she keeps hearing. The parent first asks the child what she knows about terrorists to get a sense of what the child has heard. From the child's answer here, it's clear that she knows only bits and pieces, so the parent gives a simple answer. Experts say that with children of this age, one should stop there—that is *enough*. Clinical psychologist Jama Laurent explains, "No politics. No explanations of terrorism. There's no need to get into the difference between killers and terrorists. It's our job to protect our children. There's no need to overload the little ones." However, Laurent says a parent may begin to discuss the topic in more detail with children around the age of twelve, or when they start asking more complex questions, as shown in the second example above.

Here's a question asked by children of different ages:

A four-year-old:

Child: Why did that plane blow up?

Parent: I heard it crashed. What have you heard about it?

C: I saw it blow up like *Star Wars*.

P: I saw that, too, but the plane crashed into the building. It was a very sad accident.

A five-year-old:

Child: Why did they crash the plane into the building?

Parent: There are some people who are angry. This is how they hurt us.

A seven- to nine-year-old:

Child: Why did they crash the plane into the building?

Parent: There are some very angry people in the world. And sometimes people make bad choices when they are angry, and those choices can hurt other people. It's very unfair. And it's very sad, but it can happen.

C: But why would they hurt us here?

P: There are people who do bad things. And there are people whose hatred of other people gets so out of bounds that they are willing to do terrible things that hurt other people. It does happen sometimes.

C: Will they do it again?

P: There are lots of people working to keep us all safe. The president, the military, the police officers. Mom and Dad will keep you safe here at home.

C: Why are they so angry?

P: They live in poverty in their country. We live well. That makes them angry, and they act out in anger in ways that hurt people. [Parents must fill in their own belief about why they are angry.]

These questions illustrate how to start out with very simple facts for a young child and increase in complexity to meet the needs of an older child. Michael Cohen says there is never a danger of starting out too simply. Try a very simple answer first. Read your child's cues. Does he seem satisfied with the answer? Or does he have more questions? If you start off with too complex an answer, you may confuse a child. How do you know when the answer is too complex? The child will usually look bored or tune out. After a simple answer, be prepared to keep talking, but don't feel *compelled* to keep talking. An older child will come back with more questions. If a five-year-old is asking what happened, a seven- or eight-year-old will ask "What happened?" and follow it with, "Why did that happen?" Allow a bit of silence. Wait for him to absorb the information. You can always say, "If you have any more questions about that, just let me know," or, "If you see that happen again, and want to ask me about it, we can talk some more."

A younger child:

Child: Why did they want to kill people's mommies and daddies?

Parent: There are good ways to let feelings out and bad ways to let feelings out. And terrorists let them out in very bad ways. That's why we do everything we can to keep our country safe.

A seven-year-old:

Child: Why did they want to kill people's mommies and daddies?

Parent: That's a crazy thing that happened. Most people don't want to kill mommies and daddies. Most people would never do that. But sometimes people get really bad ideas in their heads and this was one of them. If you're worried about something like that happening to Daddy or me, you don't need to worry about that. We will do our best to keep everything safe.

An older child who may want to keep talking:

Child: They're just really bad guys, right?

Parent: They let their feelings out in ways that are bad. But what do we do when we get angry or frustrated? We learn to take our anger out in ways that don't hurt ourselves or anyone else. Most people learn to do this. There are good ways of handling feelings and bad ways.

The goal with all of these responses, says Barbara Gardiner, is to zero in on the child's worry—not to impose your worries on her and not to overload her with information that is too complex. At the heart of this child's question is her fear that something could happen to her parents. Respond to her fear first with a clear and direct response: Most people would never do something like that. We will be safe, and we are doing all we can to be safe. If a child needs more of an explanation of why this happened, which may well be the case for a child over six, use this as an opportunity to explore the ways people express their feelings. You can follow this by asking the child how he expresses his anger and praising him for handling his feelings in a positive way. It's important to make it very clear, says Gardiner, that expressing feelings—however uncomfortable they may be—is a very good thing to do. Acting on them in bad or inappropriate ways is not.

Gardiner suggests saying something like, "When you're angry, you sometimes say, 'I hate you, Mommy,' or, 'Go away, I am not playing with you ever again.' That's okay. Sometimes we have angry feelings. It does not mean you are doing anything bad. Those angry feelings don't make bad things happen." Leave room for the child's own angry feelings and emphasize that *most* people who have angry feelings do not act in ways that hurt or frighten other people.

Child: Is Osama bin Laden coming here?

Parent: What have you heard about Osama bin Laden?

C: He's a really bad guy. He kills people. We're trying to get him.

P: Yeah, I've heard he's a really bad man too. Do you know any other really bad men? Who else do you know who is bad?

C: Sometimes Theo is bad and he hits me, and pulls my sweat-shirt.

P: Hmm . . . he hits you and pulls your sweatshirt. That's not very nice. Who else do you know who is bad?

C: That man . . . who takes kids away.

P: That man who takes kids away. What have you heard about him?

C: There's a bad man who takes kids away from their moms and dads.

P: Well, Osama bin Laden is not that kind of man. He does not take children away from their moms and dads. And he lives very far away, and is not in this country. What else do you think?

C: But I'm scared he's coming here.

P: You know what, sometimes that scares me too. But I say to myself again and again, Osama bin Laden is not here in America. He lives really far away in Afghanistan. And we have lots of people here in this country whose job it is to keep us safe. I just keep telling myself that.

The parent asks this child some questions about bin Laden and bad men, which allows the child to talk about his fears. What the parent discovers is that the child is not only afraid of bin Laden but of other bad guys too. He can respond to the child's more specific fear that someone will take him away. The parent shows the boy a strategy he can use to manage his fear.

Child: Dad, why do you have to fly on an airplane?

Parent: I have a meeting in Chicago and I have to take a plane to get there.

C: I'm scared. I don't want you to get on a plane.

P: I can understand why that's scary for you, but I am going because I feel it's safe. The airports have lots of people there who make sure every person is safe before they get on the plane.

C: I'm afraid your plane will blow up.

P: Our government has been working very hard to make sure airplanes are secure. And I think it's safe. And Mom thinks it's safe. Let's make a deal. Let's plan that as soon as my plane lands, I will call you and let you know I got there okay.

C: Okay. You'll call as soon as you get there?

P: I promise—remember, I have a cell phone and you can always reach me.

Children from about the ages of eight to twelve will often be most fearful of things like parents flying or planes blowing up because they have more knowledge of these incidents than younger children. However, they still lack the cognitive skills to put a rare event into perspective, and lack the coping skills that adults have. For example, they cannot yet put it out of their minds, or reassure themselves with the idea that there is an infinitesimal chance that an accident will occur. Parents can help kids by assuring them that airplanes are safer now than ever before and by making a plan to stay in touch. Let them know what time you will call, for example when you land or get to the hotel. Reassuring and providing information to the child are the two keys in calming them down. The parent at home can also help by showing the child a map of where Mom or Dad is headed and reinforcing the message that the traveling parent is safe.

Child: What's a dirty bomb?

Parent: That's a good question. It's a funny name. A dirty bomb is a bomb that spreads some nuclear material. It's very small and can only spread in a very small area. It's not going to happen here. [Depending on the details of your family's emergency plan, you can add more information, as we have below.]

P: This is why we have a safe room. It's a room that is airtight or that we can seal up to protect us from any harmful particles in the air. We don't think it is going to happen, but just in case we have a plan.

Or: Daddy and I have a plan. Remember when we bought all the extra water, and remember when you packed a backpack with toys and books? We'll take those with us so you have something to do while we wait for the news that it is safe to come out.

Child: Can I seal up my room with tape in case there's an attack?

In this case, we don't have a question, but a situation: A parent walks into a child's bedroom and discovers the nine-year-old boy sealing his closet door with Scotch tape.

Parent: What are you doing?

Child: Putting tape around my door.

P: Why are you doing that?

C: We could get attacked.

P: Really, where did you hear that? What did you hear?

C: I saw it on TV, everybody's buying tape.

P: What do you think about that? Is that pretty scary?

C: Sort of, yeah. But it's okay, we had some tape.

P: Tell me if I've got this right. You heard about the possibility of a terrorist attack, it's a little bit scary, so you've decided to put scotch tape around your closet to make it a safe place to go.

C: Yes. [Or no. If no, parent should try this again.]

P: I can see how you'd feel a bit scared. This news about terrorist attacks sometimes frightens me, too. And I can understand why you'd want to make a safe place to go. But you know, there are a lot of people all over the country who are watching very closely and working very hard to keep us safe. We're not alone. There are teachers, police officers, the president, and his staff, who are all working to help keep us safe. I'll be listening closely to the news, but if you hear anything more before I do, will you let me know? This is how I'll let you know—how will you let me know? Let's make a plan.

This boy clearly had heard some of what was in the news about increased threats of a biological or chemical attack. The suggestion by the Department of Homeland Security that Americans buy plastic sheeting and duct tape to seal off a room in their home in the event of a biological or chemical attack rubbed off on him. This boy's sense of security had been affected by the information he was getting. He was going to do what he could to protect himself.

In this conversation the parent did the following:

- Asked open-ended questions to unravel the mystery of exactly what this boy was thinking and feeling.
- Acknowledged the boy's feelings and reflected them back to the child with a summary.
- Demonstrated to the boy that the parent was really listening and wanted to be sure he got it right, by saying, "Tell me if I've got this right."
- Offered some perspective—one of the things that goes out the window when you are frightened is a sense of perspective.

In this case, the parent allowed the child to keep the Scotch tape around his closet door. It was the child's way of managing his fear, acting on it in a way that made him feel more secure. The parent then helped the boy to make a plan to give him a sense of control to the extent that that was possible. The parent also offered concrete information—which will vary according to the child's age and temperament. What's also important after a conversation like this one, in which a child expresses his anxiety, is to make sure the boy feels safe and secure. If you usually read a bedtime story, for example, make sure you do it that night. Rituals are very important to children and adults in times of stress.

Terrorism is not a threat that's going away. We may be extremely fortunate and avoid the types of terrorist attacks that have plagued other countries, but in the new global village that's something we can only hope for. And even if we never experience another terrorist attack in one of our cities, we will certainly see them, thanks to the television—right in our living rooms. As a result, we may well need to continue to rely on these basic principles: While they are very young, protect your children by giving them honest answers but minimal information. Add details in small increments. (I'll never forget the story about "spoon feeding" a child information that Tara Stackpole told me in "Conversational Comfort Zone," related earlier.) Children do not need as much information as we think they do. And we shouldn't let our anxieties push us into overinforming our children. "When kids start asking more detailed questions, then it's time to step up to the plate and answer them one at the time," says psychologist Jama Laurent. Also reassure them, as always, that you are there to keep them safe, and that there are others working hard to keep us all safe as well. As Dr. Bruce Perry reminds us, the most important thing we can do is not to color their experience with our fear: "The single most important factor is how the parent acts and reacts to the information. The more anxious, disturbed, and alarmed the parent, the more the child will cue in on this information."

A terrorist attack is meant to catch us by surprise. It's meant to make us feel vulnerable, exposed, and unprepared. Americans understand this now in a way we did not two years ago. But whether these attacks occur close to home or far away, we can be prepared to answer our children's questions with simple facts and a sense of perspective that renders the events less, not more, frightening.

Emergency Preparedness

MAKE A KIT, make a plan, and be informed." That's the advice on the home page of www.ready.go, the website of our newest government office, the Department of Homeland Security. News reports demonstrate how to seal up a room in your home in the event of a biological or chemical attack. The department's color-coded alerts establish security procedures across the country based on the risk of a terrorist attack. So far we've not yet had a "red" alert (severe risk), but we haven't had a green one (low risk) either.

New security measures at airports have us leaving our tweezers at home, packing our personal items in see-through plastic bags, and taking off our jackets, shoes, hats, belts, and anything else the new and improved federal screeners ask us to remove.

Families across the country have been making emergency plans of their own—some calmly, others in near hysteria. New Yorkers concerned about escaping Manhattan bought inflatable boats for use in the Hudson River and parked getaway cars just outside the city. A number of families built safe rooms and still more bought duct tape and plastic sheeting by the yard. I know at least one family in Los Angeles that has biochemical protection suits for themselves, their kids, and their babysitter.

And what are these families telling their kids? That varies a great deal depending on the family and the age of the children. "Anyone who shares their emergency plans with their kid is nuts," says one New York City mother of two boys, ages four and six. "Why instill that sort of fear? It does no good unless you are moving into the Annex with the Franks and if you aren't quiet, the Nazis are going to catch you and kill you. I have water, a flashlight—I even have gas masks—but I keep them tucked away in the closet. My kids don't know, don't ask, and don't care."

But some parents feel their children must be informed in order to be prepared. One mother of four older children, ages twelve through nineteen, became so concerned about another terrorist attack on New York City after September 11 that she developed a detailed emergency response plan after mapping out and personally road testing a variety of routes to a central location. After she was unable to reach her family by phone on 9/11, she even made a list of all cell phone, beeper, and office numbers, as well as e-mail addresses, and distributed it—not just to her immediate family but to extended members as well, and she insisted they carry it with them at all times. She also recommended each adult "stash" a certain amount of cash, but, as she e-mailed me recently, "I do nip into it once in a while . . . a bit too often. That is the biggest NYC problem, we are all stealing from our stash," she joked. This mother says having a plan helps her to feel that she is protecting her family and taking control. She says it gives her children a sense of security, too. They know what to do and where to go in an emergency.

The era of emergency preparedness is transforming our children's schools as well. Schools across the nation have created, reassessed, and updated their emergency plans. "Our school is eleven blocks from the White House," says Reverend Margaret Graham. "The teachers and staff all have gas masks. We have installed shades that can be pulled down to seal the windows. We have a detailed emergency plan. All the schools in the area have food and water for three days. Children have survival knapsacks with pajamas, snacks, and water. I even put big teddy bears and jars of animal crackers in the emergency kits—alongside all the gruesome first-aid sup- plies—so that the kids have something in there that's not so scary."

A school in New York City asked parents to donate bottled water. In a Washington, D.C., suburb, parents were asked to sign permission slips that allow the school to administer potas- sium iodide tablets to students to protect them from exposure to radioactive fallout from a nuclear attack. For children in other parts of the country, parents are buying readymade emer- gency kits—sometimes called "go bags"—advertised in their weekly school bulletin, or they're making them at home.

If all this doesn't freak out a parent, it would be hard to imag- ine what does. Is it any wonder that our children have lots of questions?

WHEN YOUR CHILD HAS QUESTIONS ABOUT SECURITY AND EMERGENCY PREPAREDNESS

We are raising children in a brave new world of emergency pre- paredness, a world born of the events of September 11.

Some of these new procedures can frighten children. For ex- ample, in a school on Manhattan's Upper East Side that con- verted a basement gym to a safe room, some of the elementary-school girls became very frightened at the idea that all the children would go into the basement. They'd heard that their parents would not be allowed in. If a child is frightened by security drills or plans, parents need to put things into perspective: "These are just some of the steps Mom, Dad, your school, the city, the government are taking to keep you safe. It is our job to keep you secure and we are doing our best."

Children may have lots of questions, too, about the new vocabulary of our era—anthrax, smallpox, cipro, potassium iodide, safe rooms, code orange. There are a lot of new terrors to face. Parents can use these kinds of questions as an opportunity to make a journey of discovery with a child. I call them "science project" questions. If your child is old enough, search the Web together for answers. It's a terrific resource for children and their parents to gather more information. One website I really like is FEMA.org/kids, which has sections geared toward third- and fourth-graders. It answers all their questions in a straightforward, matter-of-fact way with lots of kid-friendly graphics.

Experts say the most important message that parents can send to kids is that these are *some* of the things we do to keep you safe. As always, they say, answer your child's questions honestly and simply. But remember, every parent and every family has to do it in their own way.

• • •

QUESTIONS

"I don't want to go in the basement (safe room). Why can't our moms come get us?"

"Why are there policemen with guns on the street? Are they
   going to use them on us?"
"What is potassium iodide?"

Child: I don't want to go in the basement (safe room). Why
can't our moms come get us?

Parent: What have you heard about going in the basement?

C: At school, all the girls were talking about it. They said we
were going in the basement. And we had to stay there. And you
couldn't come.

P: There is a plan the school has. It's just like a fire drill. Instead
of going outside on the street the way you do with a fire drill,
you'll all go down in the basement. That way if there is an emergency and you can't go outside you can just go down there.

C: I don't want to go there. I want you to come and get me, and
they said you couldn't.

P: I can see how that could be scary. But I will come as soon as
the school says it's safe to take you home. They will call me on
the phone, and I'll come right away. And you won't be down
there by yourself. Your teacher will go with you, all the kids in
your class will go. And all the kids in the other classes will go
too. I'll bet it might be fun to be in the gym with all your friends
at school. Everyone will be in a very safe place together. You can
ask your teacher more about it tomorrow.

C: She's going there too? Everybody is going?

P: Yes, it's a safe place everyone goes until their moms and dads
can get there. I don't think you'll ever have to use it but I'm sure
you will have to practice going there one day just as you have

fire drills. You can ask your teacher about it tomorrow. And let me know what she says.

This child had overheard other kids at school discussing plans to take shelter in the basement in the event of an airborne terrorist attack. The parent discovered the girl's underlying fear—that she would be separated from her mother. The mother first reassured her that the basement would not be a scary place to go. It would be filled with classmates and teachers to help keep them safe. She then told her calmly that she would get there just as soon as she could. The message: This is just like a fire drill, one of the things schools do to keep you safe. They'll call the moms to come get you just as soon as they can.

This is a question a first-grader who lives in New York City asked about the heightened state of alert in New York City during the war with Iraq.

Child: Why are there policemen with guns on the street? Are they going to use them on us?

Parent: No, they're not going to use those guns on us. Policemen carry those guns to protect us from any kind of danger.

C: But I've never seen them before, why are they there now?

P: Because the situation has changed. We are in a war and when we're in a war, we take extra precautions to make sure there are no problems in the city or in the country. Putting extra policemen on the street is just one of the things the mayor and the police department in this city do to keep us safe.

C: What if somebody was going to do something bad to us?

P: Well, that's why the soldiers and policemen are here to protect us. I don't think anything bad *is* going to happen. I haven't heard that anything bad is going to happen. If I do I'll let you know.

For a child over seven provide some additional details:

P: We have a new office in our government, the Department of Homeland Security, created to protect the whole country. They tell the mayor and our city what steps they think should be taken to keep us safe. [Wait a bit to see how your child is processing this. And conclude by asking:] Does that answer your question? Or do you have some more things you'd like to talk about?

For a child over ten:

P: We have a new office in our government, the Department of Homeland Security, created to protect the whole country. They tell the mayor and our city what steps they think should be taken to keep us safe. They are working hard *to keep us as safe as they can.*

This question came up for elementary-school children in New York City during the war with Iraq. They saw a heavily armed police presence—men on the streets, in subways, and on bridges with guns. A child needs a few details to explain the facts—the men with the guns are here to protect us because we are in a war now. These times are different, so the police look different—they have different guns. With a child under ten, tell her they are here "to keep us safe." That is enough. It is one of those white lies that all of the experts I've spoken to have recommended for children under seven or eight. Of course, you are making a promise that you cannot keep. But whether the white lie is, "We do not die until we are older," or, "We are safe here at home," psychologists say the risk of you being wrong—the risk that something bad will happen—is so small that it is far better to reassure a child than it is to tell "the truth." In this instance, psychologist Barbara Gardiner recommends waiting until a child is over ten before you introduce the idea "to keep us as safe as they can." If you end the conversation, no matter how brief, by asking, "Does that answer your question?" or, "Do you have any more questions?" you keep the door open for more questions when they come up. And you let the child know it's okay to talk about all this.

Child: What is potassium iodide?

Parent: That's a good question. What do you know about it?

C: I hear they're giving it to kids in schools.

P: I know it's a medicine that protects your thyroid. Let's go search the Web and see what we can find out.

Particularly with children who are a little bit older, it's a good idea to find out what they know, reassure them that they are safe, and help them fill in information that still seems to be missing for them. Include them in the discovery process of learning more about a subject.

The best website for elementary-schoolkids I have found so far, http://fema.org/kids, answers questions about a "dirty bomb" and the threat of a nuclear attack with the following:

You may have heard the term "dirty bomb," as a terrorist weapon. A "dirty bomb" is an explosive device that scatters radioactive material. You may have also heard the term "suitcase bomb," which is a very small nuclear device about the size of a suitcase. If the U.S. government knows of a threat of nuclear or radiological attack, officials will warn residents and may advise people to take cover or evacuate. Taking shelter during a nuclear attack is absolutely necessary—below ground is best. Stay there until officials say you can leave. Talk to your parents about the location of a possible shelter and have your parents talk to your school officials, too.

Yes, this stuff is really scary—to an adult. But it does not have to be scary for children. Many of these new security precautions will be, if they are not already, old hat to our kids. The new measures at airports, for example, that we are still getting used to are a normal part of travel for our kids, who breeze through security lines without a second thought. Even new children's books, such as *Planes* from the Usborne Beginners series that I like so much, treat the new security measures and equipment as matter-of-factly as they do luggage handling, air traffic control, and food and beverage service.

In our children's schools, too, the changes will soon be familiar, if they are not already. One little girl at a Manhattan elementary school found the frozen yogurt machine empty in her cafeteria and was overheard by a teacher explaining to a friend, "I know, they took it and put it in the basement—where the safe room is—so in case of an emergency, we'll have yogurt down there." She was obviously taking the plans in stride and seemed quite reassured by the promise of plenty of frozen yogurt on hand in an emergency.

We will do our children a great deal of good by making emergency plans in our own homes to help us feel safe as long as we do it calmly and with confidence. A sense of control over our environment is an important tool for coping with fear and anxiety—for both adults and children. Emergency plans should ease our fears, not heighten them.

War

Use your words, not your hands." We spend years drilling that concept into formative young minds, teaching our children to resolve conflicts without violence. Then in an instant, admittedly a historic instant, the ultimate authority figure—the president of the United States, George W. Bush—responding to a reporter's question about Osama bin Laden, said: "I want him—I want justice. And there's an old poster out West, as I recall, that said 'Wanted: Dead or Alive.'" And with those words, the war on terrorism had begun. Just over a year later, in a special address from the White House, President Bush vowed: "All the decades of deceit and cruelty have now reached an end." He continued, "Saddam Hussein and his sons must leave Iraq within forty-eight hours. Their refusal to do so will result in military conflict commenced at a time of our choosing." Within days the United States was at war as coalition forces entered Iraq. And we were left explaining it all to our kids.

Fortunately, not too many children, as far as I can tell, spend much time or interest pondering the conflict between their parents' preaching the importance of nonviolent solutions and their country's waging war. Dr. Bruce Perry agrees: "We give our kids many mixed messages, but war does not seem to be a big conflict for most of them—violence in the name of 'good' has been glorified in our religious and secular stories, in our history books and in the familiar lore of many families with ancestors who fought in the many wars of the United States."

Children, however, are quite fascinated with the images of war, and were able to watch the war with Iraq live right in our family rooms, kitchens, and bedrooms—twenty-four hours a day. The television coverage had lots of high-tech appeal with thousands of "smart bombs" following a path from a fighter jet to buildings on the ground hundreds of miles away. In many cases, it looked just like a video game, only these were real pilots firing real ammunition. While Operation Iraqi Freedom offered the latest in high-tech weaponry, it also offered dust- and grime-covered characters—soldiers and reporters. There was plenty of action, too: Sometimes events unfolded, like the bombing of Baghdad or the toppling of the statue of Saddam Hussein, right before our eyes.

Most parents I asked about their children's reactions to the war said the same thing: This is a boy thing. One mother of two boys, ages six and two, kept her oldest son from seeing any of the war coverage. "It's too compelling for boys," she said. "They love to shoot guns. So shooting, airplanes, tanks, vehicles, things that move forward, that's what war footage is to them—cool stuff." Another mom described the reaction of her boys, ages eight and ten, to the war: "My boys have heard about Saddam's tortures—drilling kneecaps, cutting out the tongue, and various other horrors—and seem to take it in stride. War games to them seem somewhat instinctual. As a woman and a mom, that scares me a little. But then again I cry at their wrestling tournaments."

Despite the more recent war with Iraq, the war on terrorism still holds interest for many children who see Osama bin Laden as the "ultimate bad guy." One father of three boys told me: "The fourth-grade boys still all play the bin Laden game on the computer. It's on miniclips.com. Go to shoot-um-ups, and then War on Terrorism, then go to picture of bin Laden or 'killing terrorists,' and so on. They still sing a variety of bin Laden songs (one to the tune of 'daylight come and we want to go home.'— 'One bomb, two bomb, three bomb, four . . . daylight come and we drop a the bomb, come Mr. Taliban turn over bin Laden . . . six bomb, seven bomb, eight bomb, more . . . daylight come and we drop a the bomb')." If you have boys who are old enough to play on the computer you might want to check this site out.

Don't be too alarmed if your child is more fascinated with the war than frightened by the fighting or saddened by the destruction. It may just be simple, human curiosity. "It is not uncommon for kids, or for that matter adults, to become fascinated with fighting or excited when bombs explode, and they see the bright lights on television. Remember television is 'unreal' to children," says Dr. Perry. Children who respond with "fascination" are not that different from people who drive by a car accident craning their necks to get a good look. "This curiosity doesn't make a child callous or selfish. It doesn't mean the child is heartless."

Children under ten don't fully understand the concept of war, but they do understand the importance of punishment. Osama bin Laden and Saddam Hussein make perfect villains in the minds of children. They are comforted by thoughts of justice. A New York City teacher said his first-grade students, still worried about Osama bin Laden as well, were reassured by the war in Iraq. He explains, "The way they look at it is—there was a problem and somebody did something about it. We went to war. So now someone is taking care of us, we don't have to worry anymore."

But children are also worried about their safety, and the safety of their parents, whether they are serving in the war or at home watching it on TV. A second-grader from Louisiana asked his teacher: "If they kill all the soldiers in the war will my parents have to go fight?" A five-year-old boy in Denver told his parents he was afraid of growing up. When his parents asked why, the boy told them that he didn't want to become a soldier. His parents realized that the boy had seen older boys on television holding guns and thought all children would have to become soldiers when they grew up.

WHEN YOUR CHILD HAS QUESTIONS ABOUT WAR

Children's reactions to the news of war vary tremendously. Clearly a child who has a family member or friend fighting in the war will have more questions and more powerful emotions. As a result, those children will need much more support from parents, teachers, and the community. For such children, this is a difficult and stressful time. For example, at a school near Bolling Air Force Base in Washington, D.C., with many military families, teachers reported a variety of physical complaints from students, including stomachaches, while some threw up repeatedly. The teachers also saw a great deal of sadness and even despair. A six-year-old boy whose father had been deployed to Iraq from Camp Pendleton told a reporter for the *San Diego Union Tribune*: "People aren't getting along, but war is just going to make things worse. My two-year-old sister is scared. She screams for her daddy. I worry because our daddy could die. I just rock her until she goes to sleep." Children are worried about their parents, and made more anxious by the disruption in their own routine.

But even children who have some distance from the event react in very different ways. Little children, under the age of six, who don't quite grasp the concept of war will typically have very basic questions about some of the words they hear and the images they see. Older children (eight to nine) may be fascinated with the high-tech gear. Others may want to avoid the whole thing altogether, dismissing it as "boring."

With the exception of children with a family member serving in the war with Iraq, the teachers, psychologists, and parents I spoke to said there was less reaction from their children, and less fear than they had expected. The war was in a distant country, and as a result did not affect daily life for most kids. Psychologist Ruth Peters said the children in her practice did not seem particularly disturbed or anxious about the war. She did report some kids acting bored or blasé, as she put it, saying things like: "Why don't we just kill them all? It's no big deal." Peters believes that, as we learned in the chapter "Managing Your Fears," they were using their filters to keep the war from intruding in their lives.

If the country is at war, should you talk to your children about it? Many experts say with a child of four, five, or six it is too early to bring it up. "A parent's focus should be on protecting a child at that age," says Gail Furman, a child and family psychologist, rather than informing or educating. She says it's better to wait until a child is around eight years old, or until a child comes to you with questions, before you bring it up. Why eight? "That's when children can read, and have access to newspapers. They are more likely to see and hear things," says Furman. "The concept of war is more meaningful to a child of this age." As Dr. Phillip McGraw, the life strategist and television host known as Dr. Phil, put in his on-line column, *A Country at War,* "War is highly irrelevant to young children ages four, five, six, or seven. Don't make it relevant when it's not. Don't feel like as a good parent you need to sit down and talk about it. But if they've seen the images on television and have questions you do need to answer them in an age appropriate manner."

When we answer a child's questions it's important to consider that advice. When a young child asks a question like, "What does a soldier do?" or, "What's a bomb?" our minds fill with gory details. Remember, children need none of those details.

Here are just a few of the questions children have asked about some of the most recent conflicts. These questions came up during the war with Iraq, but they are the kinds of questions that kids are likely to ask about any war.

• • •

QUESTIONS

"What is a bomb?"
"What does a soldier do? Are they good guys or bad guys?"
"Are the bombs coming here?"
"Was this World War III?"

Child: What is a bomb?

Parent: What do you know about them?

C: They're like fireworks. They blow up with colors.

P: Yes, they do.

When a young child asks a question like this, ask what she knows. In this case, she was very comfortable with her own explanation. There really is no need to go any further. If you make it clear this is a comfortable thing to talk about, she'll bring it up again when she has more questions.

Child: What does a soldier do? Are they good guys or bad guys?

Parent: Well, what do you know about soldiers?

C: They wear uniforms and hats and helmets. But they're really construction workers.

P: They do wear uniforms. Oh, really, they're construction workers?

C: Yes, I saw them working on houses.

P: You saw them working on houses?

C: Yes, you know, on people's homes.

P: Really, whose homes were they working on?

C: The one with the white piano in it.

P: Oh, right, I saw that too. If you have any more questions about soldiers, just let me know.

This little boy had clearly seen the images of soldiers in Saddam Hussein's palace during the war with Iraq. And yes, there was a photo of a palace with a white baby grand piano under a crystal chandelier in the middle of a marble foyer. Because this child had clearly created his own answer for what soldiers do, and it was one he seemed quite comfortable with, there was no need to add any more information. Just keep the door open for more questions, because there will be more questions!

Child: Are the bombs coming here?

Parent: No, you're safe here in this neighborhood, and in this country. The war is in a country called Iraq. It's very far away. Iraq does not have weapons that can reach this country.

C: But I saw the bombs going off.

P: Yes, you did. That's what happens in a war. And when we see things on the news like that it can be scary. It looks like it is right next door, but the war is being fought in a place that is very far away from this country. The fighting will not come here.

This is a very common concern for children, even for children as old as ten or twelve. It is one that requires a direct, factual answer: You are safe here. The fighting will not come here. A country like Iraq does not have weapons that can reach the United States. This is a good opportunity to get out a map or a globe to illustrate just how far away Iraq is from the United States.

Child: Was this World War III?

Parent: Well, why would you think this is World War III? What do you know about world wars?

C: Well, I know that we had World War II, so is this World War III?

P: No, this was not World War III. This war took place in only one country, Iraq. And only a few countries—mainly the United States and Great Britain—fought in this war. To have a world war, many more countries must be involved.

C: Will it turn into World War III?

P: No, this is not going to be World War III. This is a war to remove a bad leader in one country from power. It is not part of a larger disagreement among countries. This war will probably be over very quickly.

This is a question a fourth-grader asked. The parent begins by asking the child what he knows about World War III. This gives the parent a chance to understand what the child has heard about world wars. If you get the sense that your child is interested, curious, or even fascinated with war, and if the child does not appear frightened, this is a good way to use your answer as a bit of a history lesson, as this parent does. The parent gives the child an honest answer and reassures him that it won't become a world war. If the child is still curious, this is a great time to help your child learn more about World War II.

As we've discussed, young children need very few details when they ask questions about war. It is our job—while they are young—to protect them from what we know are its true horrors. But for parents, the questions of war are far more complex. We have an opinion about war in general, and about each of the country's armed conflicts. On this issue, experts say to keep those opinions to yourself until your children are older, at least over the age of ten. There is no need to burden our kids with adult concerns or to raise new questions for children who are just not ready to handle them. As we've learned, children at this age think concretely and frame their world in black and white. When they are older, we can begin to add the "color" of our opinions and encourage them to develop theirs. But, again, they are just not ready for it at this age.

Afterword

As I write this we're at "orange alert" again. The Department of Homeland Security has elevated the level of risk of a terrorist attack to high. Just when life was beginning to feel "normal," we're reminded once more of that sunny fall day that changed our lives and the lives of our children forever. Nearly two years after the terrorist attacks of September 11, 2001, we're still looking over our shoulder.

Children, we've learned, are resilient, in many ways more resilient than adults. We've actually seen them—with just a bit of guidance—bounce back from life's tornadoes and move on with new strength and determination. Our children will need these skills as much as other generations have needed them, and perhaps more.

I've spent a great deal of time talking about children who are anxious, worried, and fearful. Most of the time, however, our children are none of those things. They are happy, silly, kind, filled with love and wonder. And most of all they are hopeful and good. And it's that very hope and goodness that will steer them through whatever struggles life brings.

Being a parent is beyond compare the most challenging experience I've ever had. It has also been in just these short few years the most exciting and rewarding. It is life's greatest adventure.

I started to write this book with lots of questions as a mother and a journalist. The reporter in me was looking for answers and hoping to uncover new truths. As a mother I was searching for guidance in challenging times. As a journalist, I think I've done my job. I've contacted the top experts in the field, thoroughly researched all the issues and questions. I've certainly learned things I didn't know before—always the best part of my job. And when, in some instances, the "experts" have said, "In this case there's just no definitive answer," I could examine all the arguments and lay them bare for you to examine as well. As a mother I have much less patience with this intellectual exercise. It bugs me not to have all the answers. I'm just not sure I want to rely on my instinct in times like these. But, of course, I have to. All parents do. And I have been putting a great deal of what I've learned to use, perhaps with a bit too much zeal. I've asked my son so many questions that the other day, somewhat exasperated, he said, "Why are you asking me that?"

My goal in writing this book was to help myself and if I could to share what I'd learned with other parents facing these difficult issues. Nothing would make me happier than to have the need for this book disappear. But I know that's not going to happen. So while I'll always hope that it will, I'll also know I am armed with tools I didn't have before, and some new wisdom from everyone—parents and professionals—I've spoken with over the course of this project. I have learned a great deal from them, and have been truly touched and inspired by their commitment to children. While we cannot guarantee our children a lifetime of peace or security, what we can promise them is that they'll always have a safe place to go to talk about anything, and to ask any question, no matter how frightening or upsetting it may be. We can give them a home filled with honesty, comfort, and love.

For More Information

Here are some of the books I've found most insightful, along with websites I've collected that are both easy to navigate and loaded with great information on topics such as war, terrorism, school violence, and media awareness. I've included my top picks for kids, too.

FOR PARENTS

Books

Cantor, Joanne, *"Mommy, I'm Scared": How TV and Movies Frighten Children and What We Can Do to Protect Them*. Harvest Books, 1998.

de Becker, Gavin, *Protecting the Gift: Keeping Children and Teenagers Safe (and Parents Sane)*. Dell Publishing, 1999.

Garbarino, James, and Claire Bedard, *Parents Under Siege: Why You Are the Solution, Not the Problem in Your Child's Life*. Touchstone Books, 2002.

Garbarino, James, *Raising Children in a Socially Toxic Environment.* Jossey-Bass, 1999.

Gardiner, Barbara, and Jane Aaron, *When I'm Afraid (The Language of Parenting, Part 1).* Golden Books, 1998.

Levin, Diane E., *Teaching Young Children in Violent Times: Building a Peaceable Classroom.* Educators for Social Responsibility and National Association for the Education of Young Children, 2003.

Mogel, Wendy, *The Blessing of a Skinned Knee: Using Jewish Teachings to Raise Self-Reliant Children.* Scribner, 2001.

Peters, Ruth, *Laying Down the Law: The 25 Laws of Parenting to Keep Your Kids on Track, Out of Trouble, and (Pretty Much) Under Control.* Rodale Press, 2002.

Siegler, Ava, *What Should I Tell the Kids? A Parent's Guide to Real Problems in the Real World.* Plume, 1993.

Walsh, David, *Selling Out America's Children: How America Puts Profits Before Values and What Parents Can Do.* Fairview Press, 1995.

Websites

American Academy of Child & Adolescent Psychiatry (www.aacap.org)

American Academy of Pediatrics (www.aap.org)

Children, Youth, and Families Education and Research Network (www.cyfernet.org)

Educators for Social Responsibility (www.ersnational.org)

National Association for the Education of Young Children (www.naeyc.org)

National Association of School Psychologists (www.nasponline.org)

National Institute of Mental Health (www.nimh.nih.gov)

National Institute on Media and the Family
   (www.mediaandthefamily.org)

National Mental Health and Education Center
   (www.naspcenter.org)

New York University Child Study Center
   (www.AboutOurKids.org)

Public Broadcasting System (PBS) (www.pbs.org/parents)

Sesame Workshop (www.ctw.org)

Talking with Kids About Tough Issues (www.talkingwithkids.org)
   (*Talking with Kids About Tough Issues* is a national initiative by
   Children Now and the Kaiser Family Foundation to encourage
   parents to talk with their children earlier and more often about
   tough issues like sex, HIV/AIDS, violence, alcohol, and drug
   abuse.)

Teachers Resisting Unhealthy Children's Entertainment
   (www.truceteachers.org)

Zero to Three (www.zerotothree.org)

FOR KIDS

Books

Gellman, M., and T. Hartman, *Bad Stuff in the News: A Guide to
   Handling the Headlines.* SeaStar Books, 2002.

Gellman, M., and T. Hartman, *Lost & Found: A Kid's Book for
   Living Through Loss.* Morrow Junior Books, 2002.

Websites

Federal Emergency Management Agency: FEMA for KIDS
(www.fema.gov/kids)
KidsHealth (www.kidshealth.org/kid/)
PBS for Kids (http://pbskids.org)
Sesame Street for Kids (www.ctw.org/sesamestreet)